—— **OREGON** ——
## RUNNING LEGEND
# STEVE PREFONTAINE

# ——OREGON——
# RUNNING LEGEND
# STEVE PREFONTAINE

## PAUL C. CLERICI

*Forewords by Bill Dellinger, University of Oregon coach and U.S. Olympic medalist;*
*Pat Tyson, Coach of the Year and Steve Prefontaine teammate & roommate*

THE
History
PRESS

Published by The History Press
Charleston, SC
www.historypress.com

First published 2022

*Front cover, top left*: At the 1971 AAU Track and Field Championships at Historic Hayward Field, Steve Prefontaine (254) leads Frank Shorter. *University Archives photograph, UA Ref3, University of Oregon Libraries Special Collections and University Archives UA_REF_3_A_ATHPRE0017rb*; *top middle*: Marshfield High School track in Coos Bay, Oregon. *Photo by Paul Clerici*; *top right*: Steve Prefontaine. *Photo by L.M. Harrison Jr.*; *bottom*: Prefontaine Memorial 10K in Coos Bay, Oregon. *Courtesy Coos Bay–North Bend Visitor and Convention Bureau.*
*Back cover, top*: Track Town USA in Eugene, Oregon. *Courtesy Bill Squires*; *bottom*: Steve Prefontaine, *left*, with U.S. Olympian Jesse Owens. *Courtesy The Ohio State University Archives.*

Manufactured in the United States

ISBN 9781467151733

Library of Congress Control Number: 2022936209

*Notice*: The information in this book is true and complete to the best of our knowledge. It is offered without guarantee on the part of the author or The History Press. The author and The History Press disclaim all liability in connection with the use of this book.

*I dedicate this book to my late parents, Frank Clerici Sr. and Carol Hunt-Clerici; my late brother, David Clerici; and my brother, Frank Clerici Jr.*

Steve Prefontaine, *left*, and Pat Tyson.
*Courtesy Pat Tyson.*

# CONTENTS

# FOREWORD

I was the assistant coach at the University of Oregon and Bill Bowerman was the head coach, and he could have coached Steve Prefontaine if he wanted. The first time I saw Pre run, at the state cross-country meet in his junior year in 1968, I told Bill that I saw the kid and he was going to be the next great runner. He said, "If you think he's going to be such a hotshot, then go ahead and recruit him and you can coach him."

He never missed one workout or one race in his four years-plus. That was his gift. For some reason, his body managed it all. And if you think about it, they wore leather shoes, they trained on cement, they did high and intense mileage, and they didn't have all the science we have now.

How many athletes can say they went through a whole college career and never missed a workout? And he always showed up early, too. That's what impressed me the most of all his records. He spent four years here and never missed a workout or a race. When I told him that was the record of his I liked the best, he said there were a few times when he didn't feel like running or he had a sore throat or a cold, but he knew if he told me that, I wouldn't let him run; so he didn't tell me.

I think he is the only runner in U.S. history to win the three-mile or the 5,000-meter NCAA championship four years in a row. He was a winner.

I remember in his junior year when he won the NCAA cross-country championship in Knoxville, Tennessee, in 1971. He faced one of our good young runners at the time, Garry Bjorklund of Minnesota, who had won the NCAA six-mile as a freshman. It was a six-mile race in Knoxville, which was more to Garry Bjorklund's liking than to Pre's. For strategy, I remember drills we did where Pre could run a fast three-quarter mile in the middle of a 10-mile run. He could run 3:05 in that middle three-quarter during a 10-mile run where he would run at five-minute pace; he would also finish with another fast three-quarter mile. In the middle of that 10,000, he ran a fast three-quarter, and Garry went with him. And when Pre got to the last three quarters, he had destroyed Bjorklund, and Garry wasn't able to stay with him. Pre knew how to compete in a race!

We've had a lot of great athletes here, and of all the ones that I've seen at Oregon, I don't think any of them can compare to the charisma that Pre created. He had something special between him and the crowd going that other athletes have had to a certain extent, but not to the extent that he was able to do. He would run a lap before the race, and the crowd would cheer him. And after the race, he really made the victory lap something special, waving at the crowd, shaking hands. Every time he stepped on the track, people expected him to win; and he could handle that type of pressure.

He also got in the politics of the AAU. Track and field in the United States was treated as second-class citizens, and Pre tried to change that. He was very instrumental in bringing over the Finnish team to compete and to really see America for the final meet at Hayward Field in Eugene the day he died. That was the beginning of what I think Pre would have done more of for track and field in terms of having more people recognize that nothing is being done for track and we need to be doing more.

We lost that voice for the runners when he died, but it did get picked up by a lot of runners.

I was the coach; he was the athlete. And he trusted the coaching. He reminded me of myself—an Oregon blue-collar runner, highly competitive, hated to lose. The difference between Steve and me was that he got closer to an Olympic medal faster than I did, which impressed me with him having no experience and being tough that young at twenty-one. It took me three Olympics to have the attitude that he had in his first Olympics.

I got the privilege to coach him.

—Bill Dellinger
Twenty-five-year University of Oregon coach
with 5 NCAA titles and 108 All-Americans
Three-time U.S. Olympian and
1964 Tokyo Olympic Games 5,000-meter bronze medalist

# FOREWORD

I first met Steve Prefontaine when he was seventeen, in August 1968. I was invited down from Tacoma, Washington, to watch a low-altitude elite track meet that was put on at Hayward Field in Eugene, Oregon. And Steve was invited; he was a year younger than me and was going to be a senior in high school, and I was a freshman-to-be in college. University of Oregon coach Bill Dellinger invited me, and Steve and I roomed together in a dorm on campus.

What I knew of him was only what I had read in *Track & Field News*: that he ran a state-record 9:01.3 two-mile as a junior (at the Corvallis Invitational). When I met him, I knew his name, but I didn't know how good he was going to be. He hadn't broken 8:43 yet! But what I did very well remember is that he was very ADD-like—very active, always doing something. He was definitely multitasking all the time. I never saw him take a nap.

He was a man of routine. He was religious about getting up at 6:00 or 6:30 in the morning always and religious about getting to bed before 10:00 p.m., although he might on a weekend or a Saturday night stay up later. He was a man who fixed the bed as soon as he got up. He was a man who would leave no crumb in the kitchen or dish in the sink. He liked everything clean and fresh. All bills were paid on time. I think that was from his German mother and military father.

I've met some pretty cool people in my life, even up to then, but I don't think I was ever around a person, especially that age, who was so secure and confident in himself to almost the extreme. He was very gregarious and so outgoing. I remember we went into a sporting goods store in downtown

Eugene when he was a senior in high school, and the guy there was talking about this runner named Steve Prefontaine, and Steve says, "Well, that's me!" I was just thinking that this is a pretty darn good high school runner who is sure confident in himself.

He has that…whatever *that* is.

I wasn't hero-worshipping or anything, but I grew up kind of a shy, timid guy, and I somehow drew those kinds of popular people to me for some reason. I was really lucky. I'm not real confident, but I think part of it was that I knew what to say and when to say it, and I wasn't in anybody's way. So Steve, even as we eventually became teammates and roommates, saw me as somebody who would be a really good roommate and friend. He doesn't want to be by himself, and he doesn't want to have a roommate who was going to be in his way; it's got to be the right one. It's sort of like your best friend and you just know what to say to each other and support each other.

Because Steve invited me into his life, University of Oregon head coach Bill Bowerman, for whatever reason once I was Pre's roommate, I became one of Bill's guys. Before that, I was just a runner trying to find my way, and Bill was kind of hard. But I think he was like, "Well, whatever Pre sees in Tyson, he must be all right." So after Pre and I roomed together, we became really good friends. Bill Dellinger really, really good friends to this day.

In 1971, it was Pre again as a roommate. He was the one who called me over to his trailer for dinner and said, "How'd you like to room with me?" He and his girlfriend asked me. And I said okay. I thought maybe I made a bad choice of leaving my old roommate—we had a lease on an apartment— but how do you say no to Pre? And I was not afraid of living with him either; some people might think it might be almost too much. But I looked at it as he was going to give me a lot of stuff that'll make me better.

As a student, he was a solid 3.0 student. We didn't have study halls, but he never missed a class, and he'd always sit closer to the front of the classroom because he knew that he couldn't miss anything and it would keep him awake if it was a boring lecture or something. He was very attentive, and he wanted to engage—give eye contact to the professor and be a part of it and not just sit there. I think he realized that he wasn't bright enough to just wing it. He certainly didn't take engineering classes or pre-med, but I think he knew what his passion was from the beginning, and it was communication. That particular degree would give him a lot more freedom with his running, and it's what he loved.

And he loved photography. With his photography, I'd go with him and watch him take negatives and make pictures in the darkroom. Black-and-white was what he did—a lot of nature pictures, a lot of animal pictures. He had his own darkroom and chemicals in a little shed right outside the trailer.

Also, he was involved in social justice and wanted to make a difference before it became super popular. He never talked about it; he just did it. He never brought it home. It wasn't like he'd come home and say, "Hey, Tyson, you're going to love this prison running program. Maybe you want to join me running with the inmates. Let's go to [Oregon State Penitentiary in] Salem." Or whatever it was he was doing. He never ever engaged with me the Amateur Athletic Union, the prison program—he just did it. I think maybe at home with me it was more like, "Hey, you're my roommate. I'm not going to bother you with my lifestyle." But we're going to run together, we're going to party together and so on.

He never had a brother, and even though I wasn't a little brother—I was a year older—we were brothers, and he brought me along with him and wanted to make me a better person, make me a better runner. He invited me to amazing places and to meet people like the governor of Oregon.

When I was told that he died, that was pretty tough. He had looked so young, so alive. He's one of those guys like U.S. President John F. Kennedy when he was assassinated—it's frozen in time in your memory.

When you look at when he graduated from high school, six years later he died; that was a very compact six years. Think about it; he graduated from high school, he went on the tour and met Frank Shorter and Gerry Lindgren and Rick Riley and all those other characters when he got to wear the USA jersey. Then he came in the fall and took on Lindgren and went to the NCAA and got third in his first NCAA meet because Lindgren—we call him the old man—won it and Mike Ryan was second. And then he went on and never lost an NCAA title again.

And this is with all the other things—girlfriends; photography; relationships with professors; getting connected to the prison; fighting the AAU; being a lifeguard, DJ, bartender, gas station attendant; carpentry work; being tested with a little bit of science about muscle tissue and oxygen intake; helping Bowerman find footwear, or gear even, that would be awesome to wear to give you an advantage. And he also liked to look good!

He was *the* life of the party!

—Pat Tyson
Fifteen-time Washington state champion coach,
four-time Coach of the Year
Roommate and University of Oregon NCAA cross-country championship
teammate of Steve Prefontaine

# ACKNOWLEDGEMENTS

I would like to thank all those who graciously contributed stories, photos, memorabilia, their time for interviews, and overall assistance and support in helping me make this book as rich as it is.

Thank you to Bill Dellinger and Pat Tyson for their time and their thoughtful, heartfelt, entertaining forewords. Linda Prefontaine, for caring so much. Photograph consultant Christine Lee, for her expertise and advice.

Abdi Abdirahman, ARRS, BAA (Kendra Butters, Chris Lotsbom), Steve Bence, Jeff Benjamin, Bowling Green State University, Steve Brown, Canadian Mind Products, Charleston Distance Run, Choshi City Hall Planning and Finance Department in Japan (Sasaki Yuko), Choshi International and Multicultural Association in Japan, City of Coos Bay, City of Eugene Public Works Parks and Open Space Planning (Emily Proudfoot), Frank Clerici Jr., Paul Collyer, Consular Office of Japan in Portland, The Cooper Institute, Coos Art Museum (Steve Broocks, Leah Ruby), Coos Bay–North Bend Visitor and Convention Bureau (Janice Langlinais), Coos Bay Public Schools (Sarah Eunice), Tom Derderian, Steve DiNatale, Rod Dixon, Essex General Construction (Erik Bishoff, Jodi Sommers), Eugene Police Department Public Records Office (Christopher Stetson), *Eugene Weekly* (Henry Houston), Mike Fanelli, Gerald R. Ford Presidential Library (Stacy Davis), Friendly Area Neighbors of Eugene, Zander Goepfert, Golden West Invitational (Cynci Calvin, Bob Jarvis,

John Mansoor, Bob Wright), T.K. Gore, Jacqueline Hansen, David Harrison, L.M. Harrison Jr., Jordan Hasay, Michael Heald, Julie Henning, The History Press (Laurie Krill, Hilary Parrish, Katie Parry), Bob Hodge, Molly Huddle, Carol Hunt-Clerici, Beverly Jaeger-Helton, John Kaegi, KCBY-TV, LA84 Foundation, Jean-Paul LaPierre, Barbara Lee, Stephanie Lee, Bob Levitsky, Tim Lewis, Marty Liquori, Munich Olympic Park Olympiastadion in Germany (Anja Guder, Alice Kilger, Tobias Kohler), NCAA, Nike, The Ohio State University Archives (Michelle Drobik, Johanna Meetz), Old City Artists (Erik Nicolaisen), Oregon Governor's Office of Film and Television, *The Oregonian*, Oregon Sports Hall of Fame and Museum (Jack Elder), Oregon State Penitentiary (Tonya Gushard, Stephanie Lane, Bill Marion), Oregon State University College of Agricultural Sciences Agricultural Experiment Station, Oregon Track Club, the Paddock Saloon and Grill, Pi Kappa Alpha Fraternity (Sandra Newsom), Potter Decal and Sticker Company (Dana Csakany), Steve Prefontaine Foundation, Prefontaine Memorial Run, Bill Rodgers, Charlie Rodgers, Vern Rogers, Nell Rojas, Ric Rojas, Brendan Ross, RunBlogRun, *Runner's World*, RunningPast, *Running Times*, Crystal Shoji, Frank Shorter, Sotheby's, Bill Squires, State of Oregon, Parker Stinson, Paige Stoner, Connie Stopher, Sunset Memorial Park Cemetery (Diane Morrison-Hille), Town of Glenwood, *Track & Field News* (E. Garry Hill, Tom Jordan), Track Town USA, Gigi Turgeon, U.S. Department of Agriculture Forest Service, University of Maryland Archives, University of Nebraska–Lincoln Libraries Lewis and Clark Journals, University of Oregon Libraries (Lauren Goss, Emily Haskins, Julia Simic, Randy Sullivan), University of Oregon Office of the Registrar (Bonnie Gutierrez), U.S. Selective Service System, Stuart Woods, *The World*, Dr. Eric Zemper.

For research and historical reference, I am indebted to *Best Efforts* by Kenny Moore (Cedarwinds Publishing Company, 1982); *Boston Marathon Media Guide* by BAA (BAA, 2021); *Bowerman and the Men of Oregon: The Story of Oregon's Legendary Coach and Nike's Cofounder* by Kenny Moore (Rodale, 2006); *Fire on the Track: The Story of Steve Prefontaine*, Collector's Edition (Chambers Production Corp., Oregon Production Group, 1995); *The History of the U.S. Olympic Trials: Track & Field 1908–2000* by Richard Hymans (USATF, 2004); *1972: Pre, UO Track, Nike Shoes, and My Life with Them All* by Steve Bence with Bob Welch (SB4 Press, 2021); *Out of Nowhere: The Inside Story of How Nike Marketed the Culture of Running* by Geoff Hollister

(Meyer + Meyer Sport, 2008); *Pre: The Story of America's Greatest Running Legend, Steve Prefontaine* by Tom Jordan (Rodale Press, 1997); *Shoe Dog: A Memoir by the Creator of Nike*, by Phil Knight (Scribner, 2016); *Track & Field News* (1968–1975, 2020).

# INTRODUCTION

Just like with The Beatles, whose still-reverberating seismic contribution to music and culture spanned less than ten years, so too did the duration of the impactful career of Steve Prefontaine. His iconic legacy lives on decades after his untimely 1975 death. Frozen in time, images of him locked in physically fit athletic youth, the twenty-four-year-old "rock star of running" made the most of his short existence.

Seemingly always in the national consciousness, he was nearly unstoppable in high school. Undefeated as an upperclassman, he set his first state record as a seventeen-year-old junior; as a senior, he set his first national high school record and also represented the United States in competitions against the world.

By the time he entered college, in a full-cover photo and story in *Sports Illustrated* he was pronounced as "America's Distance Prodigy." And he did not disappoint, as he won thirty-five of his thirty-eight races at his University of Oregon (UO) Hayward Field and turned in countless records, thrilling races, and exciting finishes.

A charismatic force of kinetic energy, he welcomed and relished competition and attention and rarely avoided a camera or interview. And he also made time for his ravenous fans—known as Pre's People—and routinely signed autographs after meets; often volunteered his time to help youngsters and adults alike, whether school kids or penitentiary inmates; and fought for the rights of America's track and field athletes whose success and livelihood were stymied by an archaic-thinking athletic governing body.

*Above*: Prefontaine Memorial 10K in Coos Bay, Oregon. *Coos Bay–North Bend Visitor and Convention Bureau.*

*Opposite*: Steve Prefontaine memorabilia. *Collection of Jean-Paul LaPierre.*

A legitimate medal contender at the youthful age of twenty-one, at the 1972 Munich Olympic Summer Games in Germany he finished fourth in the 5,000 meters and was subsequently favored to medal at the 1976 Montreal Olympics.

But about fifteen months before the Montreal Olympics—on May 30, 1975—just hours after he was seen fit, lively, and victorious at an international track meet he organized at Hayward Field, Prefontaine died in a car accident only a couple miles from where thousands of people last saw him compete.

News of his passing traveled worldwide.

It was not thought possible that such a young, viral, energetic life could end so tragically abruptly. At the time of his passing, he held every AR between 2,000 and 10,000 meters and two to six miles, as well as numerous high school, collegiate, state, and national records.

Interest in him has hardly waned since his passing. The rocky roadside site where he perished organically became a place to visit and pay respects and was soon referenced colloquially as Pre's Rock. The Hayward Field Restoration Meet/Bill Bowerman Classic, already previously scheduled for the week that followed his passing, was renamed in his honor as the

Steve Prefontaine Classic. Also, the commitment to create a local running trail he had championed was completed and maintained as Pre's Trail. Additionally, in his name over the years has grown a worthy list of statues, artwork, monuments, media, merchandise, sports cards, clothing, films, documentaries, a road race, a hometown tour, and other fitting honors, including numerous Hall of Fame inclusions.

Magazines in which he appeared, track outfits he wore, items he signed, and anything else connected to him during his lifetime constantly attract great interest. An autographed program from the May 9, 1975 South Coast

Steve Prefontaine magazines. *Collection of Jean-Paul LaPierre.*

International Track Meet at Marshfield High School in Coos Bay, Oregon, was appraised in 2018 on PBS television's *Antiques Roadshow* to attract between $2,500 and $5,000 at auction; and even a nondescript and unsigned racing bib number he wore in a 1970 cross-country championship meet sold for nearly $27,000 at a public auction in 2021—over fifty years later!

So many people around the world still look up to and follow his vision, his mantra, his spirit, that traveling to locations and sites where he once stood, ran, competed, lived, and visited helps bring him closer. As he was a native of Oregon, the majority of these are found in the Beaver State, primarily his hometown of Coos Bay, his collegiate city of Eugene, and his Nike connection in Beaverton. But there are other locales within the Pacific Northwest, throughout the United States, and internationally in several countries.

Accompanied with historical references to enrich the visiting and learning experience, featured here are many sites, locations, places, people, and stories associated with Prefontaine. Often shared and shown through those who knew him and those who continue his legacy, most are also supplemented with related history, anecdotal details, race and meet descriptions, finish results, addresses, and other factoids to hopefully satiate those who knew him well, inform those who do not, and aid those who recall the name but perhaps not the person.

For better organization, along with a biographical chapter, sites are situated in separate chapters for those in Coos Bay (hometown, high school, memorials, etc.); Eugene (UO, Glenwood, Salem, etc.); Hayward Field (college, post-collegiate, etc.); Beaverton (Nike, Oregon Sports Hall of Fame and Museum, etc.); Oregon movie sites (*Prefontaine* and *Without Limits*); and outside Oregon (races and events in high school, college, international, etc.). And since some races and meets lend themselves to overlap in terms of certain timeframes, some are referenced and noted as such for seasonal continuity and may be included in multiple chapters.

Enjoy visiting the many sites related to Steve Prefontaine in the hopes that through these trips, his spirit comes to life.

It is also worth remembering to please be respectful and polite when visiting any of these areas, whether indoors or outdoors.

*Chapter 1*

# STEVE PREFONTAINE

On the twenty-fifth day of 1951, Steve Roland Prefontaine was born in Coos Bay, Oregon, to carpenter and welder Raymond Prefontaine, a U.S. Army veteran, and German-born seamstress Elfriede (Sennholz) Prefontaine. The middle sibling of older half sister Neta Fleming Prefontaine and younger sister Linda Prefontaine, less than three hundred months later, on May 30, 1975, he was gone at the age of twenty-four.

Within those precious two dozen years, he was a charismatic and magnetic beacon, whether on or off the track or trail. It appeared that nothing could stop him but perhaps only himself; and while that did occur on occasion, his inner *sisu*—grit, tenacity—pushed him to prevail. Remarkably, at the time of his passing he held every AR (American record) between 2,000 and 10,000 meters and two and six miles—2,000 meters (5:01.4), 3,000 meters (7:42.6), two-mile Prep (8:41.5), two-mile outdoors (8:18.4), three-mile (12:51.4), 5,000 meters (13:21.9), six-mile (26:51.8), 10,000 meters (27:43.6)—and nine of his twelve PR (personal record) results were also ARs.

He was complex and multifaceted—friendly and secretive, vulnerable and confident, caring and brash, humorous and serious. And that was okay; he was many things to many people.

"He was a practical joker when he was a kid," remembers Linda Prefontaine. "Always enjoyed having fun and picking on me. He took competition seriously, so no messing around during races. Different story when it's over and he could relax."

*Left*: Steve Prefontaine. *Photo by L.M. Harrison Jr.*

*Below*: Elrod Street in Coos Bay, Oregon. *Photo by Paul Clerici.*

Pat Tyson, who as Prefontaine's roommate and teammate saw firsthand his intensity and fierceness when the two competed, fondly recalls his sense of humor. "I remember we'd be rolling down the highway in his little convertible, hair blowing in the wind and he's smiling. And we have AM radio on and it's playing songs from the '50s and '60s. And he's singing along, making up his own lyrics, and a lot of them were perverted," he says with a laugh. "And I would join in, and we would just trade our own lyrics, which I can't repeat," he laughs again.

As the one who introduced underclassman Prefontaine to live at the Pi Kappa Alpha ΠKA University of Oregon (UO) fraternity house in Eugene, Oregon, Gamma Pi chapter president and recruiter John Kaegi also remembers seeing the many sides of the Coos Bay kid. "Steve was one of the most liked and admired members, even as a pledge, in my four years at the fraternity. He had an aloof public persona and a reputation as arrogant and overly confident in the media. But other track teammates and competitors will tell you that he was down-to-earth, personable, yet confident. They saw his 'bragging' as humorous or comedic," Kaegi explains. "We experienced the same thing at the fraternity. I recall seeing him sitting among several older brothers in the living room, listening to music, cutting up, kidding one another, and laughing until wee hours of the night. Then, he'd arise at 4:30 a.m. and go for a run before starting his work as breakfast cook. I remember seeing him with a beer in one hand and an attractive girl—who was older than him—in the other, sitting on one of the staircases leading up to the second-floor rooms. That way, everyone would have to pass by him, which allowed him to engage them in good-natured kidding and storytelling."

It was also notable—and noticeable—how much more mature Prefontaine was even in his youthful age.

"Steve was a bit gullible and believed just about anything anyone told him. He wanted to trust people, but they often let him down," notes Kaegi. "The AAU and NCAA at the time shared—fought over—administration of U.S. track and field. Steve was first burned by the AAU the summer before he went to Oregon, and at the tender age of seventeen, he led a U.S. team protest of the AAU that eventually (years later) led to the dissolution of those arrangements and its replacement by the U.S. Olympic Committee. He was a born leader from early on, and athletes a decade older than him willingly followed him into battle."

Growing up in Coos Bay, Prefontaine attended Blossom Gulch Elementary School from kindergarten through sixth grade and Marshfield Junior High School for grades seven and eight. After less than successful

Steve Prefontaine, *left*, and Marshfield High School coach Phil Pursian. *Courtesy Linda Prefontaine/Prefontaine Productions LLC.*

junior high stints at football and basketball—largely due to his lack of size, which those sports require (he was about five feet, one hundred pounds at the time)—it was in the eighth grade when he discovered his running ability was greater than others. At a multiweek athletic program of conditioning, he improved his times in the 660-yard (1:45) and 1,320-yard (3:51) distances, and his interest grew.

In September 1965, the fourteen-year-old ninth-grade freshman joined the Marshfield High School (MHS) cross-country Pirates. Much like the connective tissue of Boston Marathon lore that binds together four-time winner Bill Rodgers, whose college roommate was 1968 winner Amby Burfoot, who was coached by 1957 winner John J. Kelley, who was befriended by unrelated two-time winner John A. Kelley, so too did Prefontaine's athletic lineage link him to the UO Ducks and the Olympics. His high school harriers were coached by two-time state champion and future MHS Hall of Fame coach Walter McClure Jr., who was coached at UO by legendary Duck and U.S. Olympic coach Bill Bowerman, whose predecessor was forty-four-year UO coach and six-time U.S. Olympic coach Bill Hayward, who had coached former UO runner and 1912 U.S. Olympian Walter McClure Sr., the father of Prefontaine's high school coach.

In freshman cross-country, Prefontaine improved enough to rise from seventh to second on the team, and he finished fifty-third at the 1965 Oregon School Activities Association (OSAA) State High School Cross-Country Championships. And in track, his mile leveled off at 5:01.

With a season under his belt, the sophomore showed great promise in the district and state cross-country meets, and he also lowered his indoor mile to 4:31. In thirteen outdoor track meets, he won the 880 yards (half mile) twice, the mile four times, the two-mile twice, and the distance medley relay (DMR) once; was runner-up twice (mile); was third only once (880 yards); and was fourth once, in the districts (two-mile). His PRs were 2:03.5 in the 880 yards, 4:29.1 in the mile, and 9:42.1 in the two-mile.

His disappointments, drive, and goal setting propelled his off-season training. The result was an undefeated junior year in cross-country (with a record-setting Oregon state title) and outdoor track (with an 11-0 record). Outdoor PRs included 1:56.2 in the 880 yards, 4:13.8 in the mile, and 9:01.3 in the two-mile, the last of which was a state record at the 1968 Corvallis Invitational Meet in Corvallis, Oregon, about a month before he won the Oregon state title in the two-mile (9:02.7).

It was around this time that his performances were attracting the attention of colleges and universities throughout the country. Bowerman sent a couple of his men to run with Prefontaine in an assessment ten-miler. And UO assistant coach Bill Dellinger, himself a 1964 Tokyo Olympic Summer Games 5,000-meter bronze medalist, first witnessed the sixteen-year-old junior Pirate at the 1968 state cross-country meet, which opened the door to UO.

Prefontaine's 1968–69 senior year at MHS was stellar, as he went undefeated in cross-country and track and set numerous records. Nearly one

Steve Prefontaine in 1967. *Courtesy Linda Prefontaine/ Prefontaine Productions LLC.*

year to the day after he set that two-mile state-record 9:01.3 as a junior at the 1967 Corvallis Invitational on April 26, Prefontaine returned to Corvallis for the 1968 edition on April 25 and by nearly 20 seconds simultaneously raised the bar and lowered the time in the two-mile to a high school NR (national record) 8:41.5.

With reportedly anywhere between three to four dozen schools interested in him—including the likes of Oregon State University (OSU), Princeton University, Stanford University, University of California–Los Angeles (UCLA), UO, University of Southern California (USC), and Villanova University—Prefontaine on April 29, 1969, signed a letter of intent to attend UO. Two months later, he made the USA National Team with his fourth-place 13:43.0 in the three-mile at the AAU Outdoor Track and Field Championships in Miami, Florida, a result that also ranked him third all-time in the high school standings.

As he headed to UO, he lived up to his pre-collegiate reputation and newspaper clippings with freshman Duck feats as winning his debut outdoor track two-mile (8:40.0) on March 21, 1970, in a tri-meet. About six weeks later, he ran a runner-up 3:57.4 at the 1970 Oregon Twilight Meet in Eugene for his first sub-4:00 mile and freshman state record, and according to "The Bible of the Sport" chronicler *Track & Field News*, he was the thirty-seventh American and seventh UO Duck to do so!

Just prior to the 1970 NCAA Outdoor Track and Field Championships, at Drake University in Des Moines, Iowa, the nineteen-year-old Prefontaine appeared on the cover of the June 15, 1970 *Sports Illustrated*, with the headline declaration "America's Distance Prodigy: Freshman Steve Prefontaine." Adding to his legend, his first NCAA three-mile title, at that 1970 NCAAs at Drake—a victorious 13:22.0 over University of Minnesota All-American Garry Bjorklund and Villanova University All-American Dick Buerkle— was clocked a few days after he reportedly cut open his foot on a jagged bolt at a diving board at the team's motel swimming pool, which required several stitches to close the wound.

Less than a week later, Prefontaine ran in the three-mile at the 1970 AAU Outdoor Track and Field Championships in Bakersfield, California. On his still-wounded wheel, he finished behind the likes of 1969 NCAA six-mile champion Frank Shorter (1st, 13:24.2), Washington State University (WSU) All-American Rick Riley (2nd, 13:24.4), 1964 U.S. Olympian Gerry Lindgren (3rd, 13:25.0), and 1968 U.S. Olympian Jack Bacheler (4th, 13:25.4), with a fifth-place 13:26.0. Disappointed at his placing, Prefontaine nevertheless made the USA National Team when the dust settled in all the events.

Historic Hayward Field. *Photo by Carol Hunt-Clerici.*

The American team competed in France, Germany, and the USSR (he skipped the U.S.-Paris meet). In Stuttgart at the U.S.-West Germany meet, he finished second (13:39.6) to 1964 Tokyo Olympic Games 5,000-meter silver medalist Harald Norpoth (13:34.6) in the 5,000 meters. And at the U.S.-USSR meet in Leningrad eight days later, Prefontaine was runner-up (13:49.4) to 1968 Soviet Union Olympian Rashid Sharafyetdinov in the 5,000 meters.

During his athletic career at UO, which spanned from 1969 to 1973, Prefontaine won seven NCAA championship titles, three in cross-country and four in track (three-mile/5,000 meters). He became the second runner to earn three harrier titles (1970-71, 1973) and the first to win four in track (1970-73). He also four times won the Pac-8 Conference Championship title in the three-mile (1970-73) and once in the mile (1971). He set all the ARs between 2,000 and 10,000 meters and between the two-mile and six-mile, as well as eight college records, with a PR of 12:53.4 in the three-mile and 27:09.4 in the six-mile.

As a Duck, he was undefeated in the three-mile, 5,000 meters, six-mile, 10,000 meters; 14 times broke his own or the AR; 9 times ran a sub-4:00 mile; 25 times ran a sub-8:40 two-mile; and 10 times ran the 5,000 meters under 13:30. His home-track advantage at Hayward Field was immense, as

STEVE ROLAND PREFONTAINE
JANUARY 25, 1951     MAY 30, 1975
COOS BAY, OREGON     EUGENE, OREGON

AMERICAN RECORDS HELD BY STEVE PREFONTAINE
AT THE TIME OF HIS DEATH MAY 30, 1975.
NATIONAL PREP RECORD
2 MILES—8:41.5, APRIL 25,-1969. CORVALLIS, OREGON
OUTDOOR
2,000 METERS—5:01.4, MAY 9, 1975. COOS BAY, OREGON
3,000 METERS—7:42.6, JULY 2, 1974. MILAN, ITALY
5,000 METERS—13:22.4, JUNE 26, 1974. HELSINKI, FINLAND
10,000 METERS—27:43.6, APRIL 27, 1974. EUGENE, OREGON
2 MILES—8:18.4, JULY 18, 1974. STOCKHOLM, SWEDEN
3 MILES—12:51.4, JUNE 8, 1974. EUGENE, OREGON
6 MILES—26:51.8, APRIL 27, 1974. EUGENE, OREGON

Steve Prefontaine Memorial monument plaque in Coos Bay, Oregon. *Photo by Paul Clerici.*

he won 92 percent of his races—35 of 38. Overall while at UO, Prefontaine won nearly 80 percent of his races—120 out of 153.

A four-time All-American, by *Track & Field News* he was listed among the top ten in the Men's 5,000-Meter World Rankings in 1971 (10th), 1972 (4th), 1973 (5th), 1974 (6th), 1975 (9th); Men's 10,000-Meter World Rankings in 1974 (10th); Men's 5,000-Meter U.S. Rankings in 1969 (3rd), 1970 (3rd), 1971 (1st), 1972 (1st), 1973 (1st), 1974 (2nd), 1975 (2nd); and Men's 10,000-Meter U.S. Rankings in 1972 (5th), 1973 (1st), 1974 (2nd), 1975 (2nd).

The Prefontaine Memorial monument plaque in his hometown of Coos Bay proudly reflects his records. And a sign of his dominance is the fact that it took forty years for someone to break the last of his major records of distances still commonly run (the three-mile and six-mile, records he set at UO, are rarely contested). At the 2012 U.S. Olympic Track and Field Team Trials on June 28, fellow former Duck Galen Rupp won the 5,000 meters in an Olympic Games–qualifying MR (meet record) 13:22.67, which beat

Prefontaine's 13:22.80 he set at the 1972 U.S. Olympic Track and Field Team Trials on July 9, 1972. Fittingly, both records were set by Ducks at Hayward Field.

Prefontaine also helped others in terms of giving his time. He volunteered at schools and colleges; coached and ran with inmates at Oregon State Penitentiary; spoke to students and runners as a much-sought-after motivational speaker at schools, camps, and conferences; and doggedly targeted the AAU, which he believed—due to its demanding, single-minded, self-serving rules and decisions—hindered American athletes' opportunities and abilities from athletic growth, being able to seriously compete against international athletes, and make a living as an athlete.

In Dr. Eric Zemper's *The Evolution of Track and Field Rules During the Last Century* presentation he delivered at the 2008 U.S. Olympic Track and Field Team Trials at UO, the then-IAAF international technical official explained that the rules against which Prefontaine fought were six decades old, dating to a report at a Special Committee on Amateur Statute meeting.

"The rules governing amateurism adopted by the new IAAF in 1913 had as their first principle, 'An amateur is one who competes for the love of the sport.' The second principle was, 'Competing for money or any other pecuniary [money-related] reward in any sport makes the competitor a professional in all sports.' And third, 'In track and field athletic sports, one who knowingly competes with, or against, a professional, thereby becomes a professional.' This is the infamous 'contamination rule.' The IAAF also declared that anyone who taught, trained, or coached any sport for money was a professional, although they did allow each country to decide on this issue for domestic competition," he stated. "Among other parts of the amateur regulations was the requirement that 'an amateur may not sell, pawn, or give away' any prizes earned, and 'shall hold the same subject at all times to the inspection of the member of the federation of his country.' Also, there was a stipulation that any expense money paid for an athlete's travel, housing, or meals must be paid not to the athlete but to a member of the federation of the athlete's country."

Zemper also included in his presentation Prefontaine's 1970s battle with the AAU over its decades-long stronghold in relation to athletes' ability to make a living while training and competing.

"Sixty years later, this was one of the rules that Steve Prefontaine and others were fighting with the AAU about, and that eventually helped lead to the [1978] federal act stripping the AAU of its control of sports in this country, and led directly to the formation of The Athletics Congress, now the USATF. But over a century ago, sports like track and field were seen as a gentlemanly pursuit of the more privileged class that must not be sullied by the pursuit of money, and those who set themselves up in control did everything they could to see that it remained that way," he presented.

To earn enough money to just stay afloat and continue their elite-level training, proper athletic nutrition, and high-end competition, athletes circumvented AAU rules in races where they were paid "under the table" by race officials or other organizers or, in some instances, accepted a job that in the AAU's eyes still flirted dangerously close to ineligibility, like Prefontaine's reported $5,000-a-year "stipend" from Nike. But, for various reasons, Prefontaine did turn down a reported $200,000 pro contract from International Track Association, which organized a circuit of meets from 1973 to 1976.

Still, Prefontaine received from the AAU notices of concern whenever it learned he received clothing, running shoes, payment, and so on. All this as the AAU expected athletes, under its restrictive guidelines, to nevertheless support themselves between Olympic Games! In addition, the AAU also determined where and against whom an American track and field athlete would compete, regardless of talent level and, again, with no benefits for their efforts.

These limitations enraged many, especially Prefontaine, who realized that to beat the best in the world you had to compete against the best in the world. He had also experienced this firsthand when he competed in West Germany and noticed the less-than-ideal conditions in which the American athletes were housed compared to those from other countries via their federations and governing bodies.

While his own athletic success primarily resulted from his hard-fought, take-charge, front-running ability, there were times when he suffered from that AAU mandate when he competed against runners who employed an international style to racing that he was rarely permitted to face. Whenever he ran against the likes of a Filbert Bayi of Tanzania, Rod Dixon of New Zealand, Norpoth of Germany,

Steve Prefontaine Nike running shoes.
*Photo by Paul Clerici.*

Emiel Puttemans of Belgium, or Lasse Viren of Finland, for instance, he was not always the automatic favorite. Nor always the winner.

One of those international runners who beat Prefontaine a number of times, and whose competitive relationship eventually grew to an overall friendship, was Dixon. Born in July 1950, only six months separated the two as on opposite sides of the globe—and training and governing-body support—they ascended on their respective meteoric rises.

"When Pre and I raced in London [after each having set records], as you do you congratulate one another. And he said to me, 'You sit on me and I'll…give you a prick on your ear,'" Dixon said with a laugh at the recollection of the pre-race banter. "And I said, 'Hold on, hold on. It's not about personality. You've got to learn, Steve, you've got to race the people. You're not racing in Eugene anymore; you're racing in the world. This is Europe; we're not going to do what you want us to do.' But I'll tell ya, he was tough. I remember it was four days before a [European two-mile] race, and Pre did a two-by-one-mile, 10-minute recovery, and he ran 4:02 and 3:59.3, with 10-minute recovery! That suited him! Pre was tough. But the one thing he didn't do was that he had to get on and get to Europe if you're going to improve. And you've gotta have that 'have bag will travel' [attitude]."

Shortly after his fourth-place finish at the 1972 Munich Olympic Summer Games 5,000 meters, for example, Prefontaine faced Dixon in September at the 1972 Coca-Cola International Meet two-mile in London, England, at the Crystal Palace. With a strategic approach, while not pushing a front-running pace à la Prefontaine's style, Dixon won in a UK All-Comer's record 8:19.4 to Prefontaine's second-place AR 8:24.8.

"After the Munich Olympics, I was stepping up from the 1,500 meters to the two-mile and Prefontaine was stepping down from the 5,000 meters to the two-mile," Dixon said. "During the warmup, I did note that he and I acknowledged one another. I didn't have any conversation after the event, other than to say congratulations. And he virtually ignored me by saying all I did was sit on him and [that] I and nobody [else] contributed to the pace and race. Other than that, there was no conversation. I felt it was an aggressive response to my congratulations. And others did note the attitude."

Dixon also beat Prefontaine at the 1974 Milan International Meet 3,000 meters at Arena Civica in Milan, Italy, where his NR 7:41.0 beat Prefontaine's runner-up AR 7:42.6.

"[New Zealand two-time 1974 British Commonwealth Games medalist] John Walker and I traveled to Milan for the international track meet. We all lined up, the gun went off and [Franco Fava] led out for the first 400 meters, and then Pre took over and started to push the pace. I moved up and behind him at that point, and I knew the pace was fast. At four laps to go, I took over from Prefontaine and started to push the pace even more. Each time he came up beside me to take the lead, I sped up, and it was kind of like that for the next two and a half laps. With 350 meters to go, he sprinted past me and left me with much surprise; however, I was able to crawl back the gap. And as we turned into the home straight, I came alongside him and we were stride-for-stride for the next 10 to 20 meters and then I lifted again to win the race. Pre came over, and suddenly all the past [contention was] all behind us, and we agreed we would be great friends."

Friendship did indeed grow from that race, which, as far as Prefontaine was concerned, showed Dixon's approach to racing mirrored his own in terms of attack and guts as opposed to resting back and surging late after someone else does all the work. The three of them—Dixon, Prefontaine, and Walker—found themselves bonding afterward on and off the track.

"Yes, after the Milan 3,000 meters, we were at the hotel having a few beers and a few more, and we started to realize we were in for 'a session.' We agreed that no matter how many beers we would have, we're still going out for our run in the morning at 7:30 a.m. and we were going to do a ninety-minute run. After about ten beers we [knew that was enough and] said, 'Right, 7:30 in the lobby,'" recalled Dixon. "For ninety minutes [the next morning], we ran at near-race speed. Walker would push the pace, I would rest; I would push the pace, Walker would rest. *Not* Pre! He kept responding to every surge. After that training session, we had a certain respect for each other. And we then realized we were equal and [one of us] was not going to dominate the other. I think John Walker and I also announced to Pre that he was now officially an honorary New Zealander."

About two weeks later, on July 18, in the two-mile at the 1974 July Games in Stockholm, Sweden, Dixon won again in a NR 8:14.4, with Puttemans second (8:16.6) and Prefontaine third (AR 8:18.4). And in the mile at the 1975 *Los Angeles Times* Indoor Track Meet, at The Forum in Inglewood, California, the top five finishers were Bayi first (3:59.6), Walker second (3:59.9), Dixon third (4:01.1), Byron Dyce of Jamaica fourth (4:01.3), and Prefontaine fifth (4:03.4).

"At the one-mile at the *Los Angeles Times* indoor track meet, we were focused on all of us breaking the four-minute mile," says Dixon, who further added that Prefontaine also wanted to partake in some of the international training that Dixon and Walker enjoyed.

"It was at this meeting we discussed the plan for Pre to come to New Zealand to train in New Zealand summer [October through February] in preparation for the 1976 Olympic Games. Pre liked the idea to have two effective 'year' summers in which to prepare for the Olympics while not having to withstand the cold winter conditions of the Northern Hemisphere. He realized what we had discussed is that we New Zealanders had two summers a year [that enabled] us year-round training," noted Dixon. "And that we—John Walker and I—would join Pre and his training program location he was setting up in Boulder, Colorado, and that we would share his property with him and we would all train towards the Olympic Games."

On his own, Prefontaine embarked on what the AAU did not: competitions against the world's best, whether that entailed seeking out runners and meets himself or bringing them to the United States. All the while, he did not shy away from sharing the fact that he was living on food stamps and three-dollar diems from the AAU. He also made it clear that he was not the only one.

Prefontaine focused on many things after the Olympics: pressuring the AAU; bringing international athletes to compete in the United States; spreading the word about a new brand of running shoes called Blue Ribbon Sports and then Nike; training for the 1976 Montreal Olympic Summer Games; and other endeavors.

However, tragedy occurred on May 30, 1975, when he died in a car accident on a short and winding road just outside UO at the age of twenty-four. His death affected many, perhaps more than he would have ever imagined.

The last time Dixon competed against Prefontaine was in the mile on February 7 at the 1975 *Los Angeles Times* Indoor Meet in California, just over three months earlier.

"After the [1975] *LA Times* track meet and a couple beers, we said our goodbyes, as John Walker and I were heading off for a couple more races and then back to New Zealand. We continued to communicate during the month of March and April and making plans for his travels to New Zealand," Dixon recalled of his last conversations with Prefontaine. "I was absolutely devastated May 30, 1975, when I got a phone call to say that Pre had been killed in a car accident just after the USA-Finland track meet. Absolutely devastated. Pre and I [first] raced in 1972. A few beers and a few years later, we started to let our guard down. Of course, in '73, Pre, Walker, and Dixon got on really, really well," Dixon added with a comforting laugh. "It was fabulous. We used to do these runs, and one of the first or second runs we would test each other, as you do. I would test and John would test, and Pre would show, 'Well, I can do this, too.' And you'd come back after a two-and-a-half-hour run, and it was close to marathon race pace the whole way, and we're going to beat each other up if we continued to train like this. So we had a few beers and we talked about it. He was tough."

News of Prefontaine's passing quickly traveled worldwide and even reached the White House. Shortly after the death of their son, his parents received a letter of condolence from U.S. President Gerald Ford.

Obtained through the Gerald R. Ford Presidential Library, the June 5, 1975 letter reads: "Dear Mr. and Mrs. Prefontaine, Mrs. Ford and I were deeply saddened to learn of the tragic accident which took the life of your son, Steve, and we want you to know that you are very much in our thoughts and prayers at this time. Throughout his athletic career, Steve accumulated a great many honors, as well as a multitude of friends and fans. He was admired as much for his determination, courage, and competitive spirit as for his outstanding ability as a distance runner. We hope the knowledge that your sorrow and sense of loss is shared by your fellow citizens will serve to comfort you in the days ahead. Mrs. Ford joins me in extending our deepest sympathy to you and your family. Sincerely, Gerald R. Ford."

One of the first sparks of his posthumous legacy began as the Steve Prefontaine Foundation, started and fueled by Jon Anderson, Wade Bell, Bowerman, Roscoe Divine, Greg Foote, Jim Grelle, McClure, Kenny Moore, and Raymond Prefontaine. Initial advocacies included a trail for runners, eventually named Pre's Trail; financial support for young athletes, primarily females, for whose rights Prefontaine fought; to improve and replace high school and community tracks throughout Oregon; and to help keep the fire to the feet of the AAU.

Regarding the AAU in the years prior to Prefontaine's passing, groundwork had been laid to address the myriad issues. In front of the U.S. Senate, in March 1973, U.S. Senator Marlow Cook of Kentucky introduced "a bill to establish a Federal Amateur Sports Commission. Referred to the Committee on Commerce."

As Senator Cook stated, in part, according to the March 13, 1973 public U.S. Congressional Record of the 93rd Congress, "There is little reason to burden this Record with documented evidence of the confused state of affairs which our talented athletes are forced to face. The large number of rules and regulations with which these men and women are forced to comply serve only to handicap their pursuits and stifle their development and success. The situation is crystal clear—the amateur sports hierarchy, riddled by divisiveness, is not functioning in the best interests of the athletes. Rather, that hierarchy has become a self-perpetuating, self-aggrandizing system which seriously jeopardizes the ability of the United States to field representative teams in international competition."

His comments echoed what Prefontaine and others had been preaching for years—so much so that Senator Cook included him in his presentation to the Senate: "Olympic hurdlers have sometimes been forced to train with only one hurdle at their disposal. The training table for some of our athletes at the [1972] Olympic Trials, according to Olympian Steve Prefontaine, has been 'the corner hot dog stand.' It is time that this body endeavor to correct this problem which the rules of amateur sports in this country cannot even see."

Two months later, the U.S. Senate Committee on Commerce, on June 27, 1973, "voted to report the Amateur Athletic Act of 1973, a bill designed to protect the rights of our amateur athletes in athletic competition, and to provide the foundation for better training, better coaching, and better facilities for amateur athletes," stated U.S. Senator John Tunney of California.

The Amateur Athletic Act of 1973–Amendment was presented to the U.S. Senate at the August 3, 1973 session by Senator Tunney, on behalf of himself and fellow senators Cook, Mike Gravel of Arkansas, Warren Magnuson of Washington, James Pearson of Kansas, and Strom Thurmond of South Carolina. He also included in the U.S. Congressional Record the Statement of Olympic Athletes, which stated, in part, "We welcome the recent efforts designed to foster the development of sports by insuring [sic] the participation of athletes. This legislation alone is not the solution: there is no single solution. But it is a well-conceived beginning, and it deserves to become a first step."

Among the forty-eight U.S. Olympians who signed the Statement of Olympic Athletes were 1960 Rome Decathlon gold medalist and 1956 Melbourne Decathlon silver medalist Rafer Johnson, 1964 Tokyo 10,000-meter gold medalist Billy Mills, two-time U.S. Olympian Kenny Moore, two-time U.S. Olympian H. Browning Ross, 1960 Rome three-time gold medalist and 1956 Melbourne bronze medalist Wilma Rudolph, three-time U.S. Olympian and 1968 Mexico City silver medalist Jim Ryun, 1972 U.S. Olympian Steve Prefontaine, and 1972 U.S. Olympian Steve Savage.

After years of much debate and discussion by many people, three years after Prefontaine's death the Amateur Sports Act of 1978 was signed into law by U.S. President Jimmy Carter. Also known by the cumbersome title "An Act to Promote and Coordinate Amateur Athletic Activity in the United

Steve Prefontaine autograph. *Collection of Jean-Paul LaPierre.*

States, to Recognize Certain Rights for United States Amateur Athletes, to Provide for the Resolution of Disputes Involving National Governing Bodies, and for Other Purposes," it essentially disassembled the AAU and created the U.S. Olympic Committee, which establishes each sport's individual governing body. Twenty years later, the Ted Stevens Olympic and Amateur Sports Act, a 1988 revision named after the Arkansas senator, added other measures important to Prefontaine, including that "amateurism is no longer a requirement for competing in most international sports."

Shorter—a two-time U.S. Olympic medalist and former U.S. Anti-Doping Agency chairman who also has a law degree—battled the AAU side by side with Prefontaine and recalled personally witnessing injustices.

"We knew in 1969. But the idea started when Steve and I, and some other guys, were at a meet in Italy in 1974 and there was an Italian runner we knew who came up at the end of the meet and said, 'Let's get our money and go celebrate.' And we said, 'What money?' We were running for the U.S., and the U.S. was getting our appearance money," he noted. "We all made these international teams and went with them because it was the only way you could get to Europe to run. You had to be on a USA team because if you went to a foreign country, you would have to have from our federation a travel permit that verified your amateur status. If you didn't, you couldn't run there as an individual. So they used that as a lever to get people to be on the national teams. That's why we were on the national teams. And when we would barnstorm around Finland, we just sort of ignored that, and fortunately the coaches and everybody ignored that, too, and the federation knew they were making enough, so wink-wink, we'd look the other way. So what we had to work on first was to do away with that so we could go over there independently, when it really would matter."

Shorter recalled one of the major keys to success was forging relationships with those who could make a difference, such as politicians, leaders, and so on.

"It has to be step by step, and the time has to be right; there has to be a window," he said. "And you have to make friends and gain trust and build up the trust with the people [who can help]. It has to be the top down; you have to find people as high up as you can to work for you. You just have to convince somebody who has the power."

What was it that drove Prefontaine to such battles against what he felt was unjust?

"Determination!" declares Linda Prefontaine. "Fairness for all! [He] understood that he had the power to change the world."

He did take a stand when he saw a need, whether it was voicing his opposition against the sport's governing body to help the American athlete; speaking in front of the Oregon State Senate in regard to farm burning and its related hazards to air quality; or letting it be known of his support for his fellow Black teammates at UO.

"Most voices are quiet," notes Tyson, "and there's Steve who was outspoken—much like his coach Bill Bowerman; outspoken with the Wild, Wild West mentality. He had it, and he was real proud of it. [With the AAU,] that was part of everything that was going on with the injustice, the civil rights movement, the Vietnam War—and here's Steve. We were at Oregon with a liberal arts education, and our professors wanted us to be activists. And being in journalism and communication, these guys…I remember him sitting in church, and I was at that church, and U.S. Senator Wayne Morse [of Oregon] speaking about [issues and causes]. Here we are at church, and it's like Boston, Massachusetts, during the Revolutionary War with citizens in churches talking about protesting and boycotting and civil unrest and what we can do to make a difference. That was Eugene, Oregon!"

The period during which Prefontaine was at UO—from 1969 to 1974—was filled with great unrest and change in the country. It was a nation living in the aftereffects of killings of such leaders as NAACP civil rights activist Medgar Evers (1963), U.S. President John F. Kennedy (1963), civil rights activist and musician Sam Cooke (1964), human rights and civil rights activist Malcom X (1965), the Reverend Martin Luther King Jr. (1968), U.S. attorney general Robert F. Kennedy (1968), and Black Panther Party leader Fred Hampton Sr. (1969).

That five-year span also was a time of the Vietnam War (1955–75); the fatal shootings at Kent State University in Ohio (1970); the Watergate political scandal, investigation, and presidential impeachment and resignation (1972–74); sit-ins, demonstrations, protests, and marches; and general distrust of authority and government.

UO was not immune, of course, as it had its share of demonstrations and destructions, some of which included the student "occupation" of Johnson Hall; an arson fire at Esslinger Hall's storage area of its ROTC; and a bomb detonated at Prince Lucien Campbell Hall.

"He did keep a low profile in the summer of '72," Tyson recalls of Prefontaine. "Of course, we had a presidential election with George McGovern and Richard Nixon. And he never voted. That would have been the very first time that he would have been able to vote. He didn't really share a lot about his thoughts about the war or politics. Some people always ask me why, and I don't think he wanted to get too involved because it would take away from his focus on what he was trying to do. I was much more politically active than him, probably because my mother told me I better frickin' vote! I was the one that put bumper stickers on my car that said, 'Don't blame me, I voted for McGovern' or 'Nixon peace plan—the bomb.'"

When it came to civil rights and supporting people of color, Prefontaine and his teammates stood by each other.

University of Oregon 1970s track patch worn by the athletes. *Courtesy Pat Tyson.*

"Growing up in blue-collar white Coos Bay and coming to white Eugene, here we have a team of mixed races, and that was what Bowerman was all about—inclusion—and we, including Steve, were all part of wearing little emblems on our track gear that had what was called 'Afro Duck' and a regular Duck," notes Tyson of the ubiquitous Fighting Duck mascot logo of UO, which was altered to make a point. "That was symbolic of 'We are united,' kind of an ebony and ivory, before that [Paul McCartney–Stevie Wonder] song came out. It was part of who we were. You can see it

*From left*: Three-time USA National Team coach Mike Fanelli, 1976 U.S. Olympian and Steve Prefontaine teammate Paul Geis, 1964 U.S. Olympic bronze medalist and Steve Prefontaine University of Oregon coach Bill Dellinger, four-time Coach of the Year and Steve Prefontaine University of Oregon teammate and roommate Pat Tyson. *Courtesy Mike Fanelli.*

if you look at a couple of the shirts that Pre was wearing; and even on the back of his MG was a decal of 'Afro Duck.' So if anybody wants to know about a guy who was all about inclusiveness and Black Lives Matter, that was Steve, too."

UO's Duck mascot replaced the school's original nickname, Webfoot. A 1700s reference to New England fishermen whose trade kept them in wet environs, it remained with those from the East Coast who transplanted to 1840s Willamette Valley, and in time, the state of Oregon itself adopted the moniker. When the name Duck began to stick from constant usage due to its ease of use by sportswriters and colloquially, the next step was a mascot image, and Walt Disney's Donald Duck fit the bill. Since 1947, various agreements have been struck between UO and Walt Disney Productions.

In 1971, UO's track and field athletes wanted a change to reflect their support of each other, and a Black hurdling Duck was created by Quintin Barton of the Potter Manufacturing Company in Eugene, Oregon. While the image of a Black Duck with an afro hairstyle is considered stereotypically politically incorrect today, at the time it was used to express support. In addition, a twin Duck logo patch that featured a Black Duck athlete alongside a white Duck athlete was worn on uniforms. Soon thereafter, the Black Duck was incorporated for the basketball team, and eventually, other schools contacted Potter Manufacturing for their own mascots.

"He didn't judge anybody," said Tyson of Prefontaine.

In addition to the many honors and accolades in his name, including a Eugene Symphony world premiere performance of the "Prefontaine" composition in 2022, he has also been inducted into the USATF National Track and Field Hall of Fame (1976), RRCA Distance Running Hall of Fame (1981), Oregon Sports Hall of Fame and Museum (1983), UO Athletics Hall of Fame (1992), National Distance Running Hall of Fame (2000), NHFS Sports Hall of Fame (2000), MHS Athletics Hall of Fame (2003), and the inaugural USTFCCCA Collegiate Athlete Hall of Fame class (2022).

*Chapter 2*

# COOS BAY, HOMETOWN, HIGH SCHOOL, MEMORIALS...

S teve Prefontaine's birthplace of Coos Bay, Oregon, was founded in 1853—six years before Oregon became the thirty-third state—and was incorporated in 1874. It was originally named Marshfield, after founder J.C. Tolman's Massachusetts hometown. In 1944, Marshfield became Coos Bay, in which is located the headquarters of the federally recognized Confederated Tribes of Coos, Lower Umpqua, and Siuslaw Indians (CTCLUSI).

Prior to the founding of the Northwest Plateau, Indigenous people called Coos lived there and spoke in the languages Hanis and Miluk. Indications regarding the word *Coos* seem to derive from *kuukwis*, the Hanis and Miluk word for "south," to reference themselves as being south of the Siuslaw and Umpqua people who lived north of them. Later, according to CTCLUSI, it was during Captain Meriwether Lewis and Second Lieutenant William Clark's 1805-06 portion of its Corps of Discovery Expedition where is found the first written mention of Coos, in a journal list that includes "Cook-koo-oose Nation" in reference to the Coos Indigenous people.

The tough, focused, resilient folks of Coos Bay are forged by the expectation of honest labor in the difficult commerce of the hardworking industries of lumber and fishing; the required need to survive varying seasons; and the ability to adapt and succeed. One of the areas where these attributions are beneficial is on the proving grounds of sports. For Prefontaine, that became track ovals, race courses, and cross-country trails.

Entering Coos Bay, Oregon. *Photo by Paul Clerici.*

Coos Bay, Oregon. *Photo by Paul Clerici.*

He was born in small-town Coos Bay in 1951, inside McAuley Hospital, located at the corner of Commercial Avenue and North 8th Street (later known as Ken Keyes College at 790 Commercial Avenue, it was torn down in 2018). According to the closest U.S. Census Bureau count, in 1950, the population of Coos Bay was just over 5,900 (tripled to 15,985 by 2020).

His primary and lower secondary education (kindergarten to grade eight) was at schools whose locations, grade levels, and/or mascots have since changed. He attended the pre-Panther days of Blossom Gulch Elementary School, then kindergarten through grade six at 333 South 10th Street. (While students moved to other buildings by 2020 as part of a plan to replace the school, it was later used as a temporary facility during other construction and planning delays.) His intermediate school was Marshfield Junior High School, for grades seven and eight, at 755 South 7th Street (then known as the Redskins, the mascot was changed to Buccaneers).

He lived his formative years at the publicly noted 921 Elrod Street family house that his father, Raymond Prefontaine, built in 1961 (not 1963, as erroneously marked on a site plaque). As Linda Prefontaine recalled, "My dad built our first house in Englewood before we were born. When we were still under the age of six, we moved closer to downtown. While my dad was building the house on Elrod, we lived in a couple of rentals."

Elrod Street in Coos Bay, Oregon. *Photo by Paul Clerici.*

Prefontaine Memorial 10K in Coos Bay, Oregon. *Courtesy Coos Bay–North Bend Visitor and Convention Bureau.*

Family matriarch Elfriede Prefontaine—who passed away in 2013, nine years after her husband, Raymond, died in 2004—often greeted runners from their Elrod Street front yard during the annual Prefontaine Memorial Run 10K road race. The course includes parts of Elrod, and Elfriede and Linda would cheer on and high-five runners as they stopped to say hello during the race.

First run in 1980, it is detailed on the race website as "a rolling, challenging course along one of Steve's favorite training routes." It starts in downtown, proceeds westward along Ocean Boulevard, then Elrod Street past the family home, and finishes at the high school track. A separate 5K and two-miler were later added. The races, whose fields on average attract several hundred participants, are part of the Bay Area Fun Festival, a three-day event in the fall that features performances, food courts, entertainment, music, a parade, and other family activities.

According to a Prefontaine Memorial Run race application, "Those special qualities that made Steve Prefontaine a hero to track fans [during his lifetime] are still creating new admirers. Many who were not born when Pre was setting records, or ever saw him compete, are inspired by his enduring example of courage, feisty determination, and charisma. [This] popular run got its start when a group of Coos Bay citizens decided it was time that Steve Prefontaine's hometown did something to honor its favorite son."

He attended Marshfield High School (MHS) at 972 Ingersoll Avenue, where as a Pirate he began to truly flourish as an athlete on his home track inside Pete Susick Stadium, named after the school's longtime legendary football coach. This is where the world began to take notice of the youngster's exploits, as early indicators heading into his 1965-66 freshman year included a 1:45 in the 660 yards and 3:51 in the 1,320 yards.

As a frosh harrier, by season's end he had jumped five positions to the number-two spot and finished fifty-third in the Oregon School Activities Association (OSAA) State High School Cross-Country Championships. In track, he lowered his mile to 5:01.

In his sophomore year, while Prefontaine did not win the 1966 district cross-country meet, a sign of things to come in regard to his athletic ability shined even more brightly with a gutsy run over the majority of the race; people took notice of the budding talent. Also, his indoor track mile improved to 4:31. And in his 1967 outdoor track season, he recorded PRs of 2:03.5 in 880 yards on April 15, versus Roseburg High School; 4:29.1 in the mile on May 11, at the SCJV meet in Coos Bay; 9:42.1 in the two-mile on April 4, at Reedsport High School in Oregon; and 4:32.1 in the distance medley relay (DMR) on April 5, at the Spike Leslie Relays in North Bend, Oregon.

While his underclassmen years featured spots of greatness and a promising trajectory in terms of improvement and skill, his goal-setting focus, and determination—coupled with eventual two-a-days, seventy- to seventy-five-mile weeks, and the continued guidance and coaching from Walter McClure Jr. and Phil Pursian—led to a breakthrough and attention-getting 1967-68 junior year.

Undefeated in cross-country, Prefontaine, now standing at five feet, nine inches and about 140 pounds, won the 1967 OSAA State Cross-Country title, the championship meet of which was personally witnessed by University of Oregon (UO) Ducks coach Bill Dellinger, whose observations would eventually lead to the Pirate becoming a Duck.

In his 1968 outdoor track season at MHS, whose home surface was cinder, Prefontaine's PRs included a 1:56.2 in 880 yards on May 10, versus North Bend; the state's fourth-fastest mile (4:13.8) on March 23, at the Indian Club Relays in Roseburg; state-record 9:01.3 in the two-mile on April 26, at the Corvallis Spartan Invitational Track Meet at Corvallis High School in Oregon; and a 4:21.1 in the DMR on April 4, at the Spike Leslie Relays.

Marshfield High School in Coos Bay, Oregon. *Photo by Paul Clerici.*

Prefontaine's 1968-69 senior year was a quantum leap that began with another OSAA State Cross-Country Championship. He started his 1969 outdoor track season with an undefeated slate of doubling and tripling in meets where he won the 880 twice (including his high school PR 1:54.3), the mile three times, the two-mile once, and legs in the mile relay, sprint medley relay (SMR), and DMR, in four meets in March and April.

The main goal of the season was to peak by the end of April in time for the 1969 Corvallis Spartan Invitational Track Meet at Corvallis High School, 1400 Northwest Buchanan Avenue, in Corvallis, Oregon. His focus was on the three-year-old two-mile record of 8:48.8 set by Ferris High School's Rick Riley of Spokane, Washington, at the 1966 Washington State Meet.

Prefontaine entered the race with his two-mile PR of 9:01.3, the Oregon state record he set in Corvallis nearly a year to the day earlier, on April 26, 1968. While he also ran a 9:02.7 two-mile at the 1968 state high school meet at Corvallis, his most recent two-mile prior to the 1969 Spartan Invitational was a 9:13.4 at home versus Oregon's Grants Pass High School about three weeks earlier, on April 5.

At the Spartan Field track on April 25, 1969, Prefontaine led at the first mile in 4:25, ahead of Oregon's Doug Crooks of North Eugene High School, who the week before had run the year's national best two-mile in

9:03. Seemingly in charge throughout the contest, though, Prefontaine turned in laps of 66, 65, 64, and a 61.5 bell lap for a 4:16.5 second mile and new high school NR 8:41.5. With his convincing run over Riley's mark, those outside Coos Bay and parts of Oregon began to take notice of the eighteen-year-old phenom.

After a few more regular-season meets, Prefontaine continued his dominance at the district meet in Springfield, Oregon, on May 23, where he won the mile (4:07.4) and two-mile (9:14.3); 1969 Oregon State Meet in Corvallis on May 30, where he again won the mile (4:08.4) and two-mile (9:03.0); Golden West Invitational in Sacramento, California, on June 14, where he won the mile in his high school PR (4:06.0), which put him at number ten on the all-time high school rankings list and behind only 1969 Minnesota State Meet 4:05.1 miler Garry Bjorklund of Proctor High School for the year's best; 1969 AAU Outdoor Track and Field Championships in Miami, Florida, on June 29, where his fourth-place three-mile 13:43.0—his high school PR—was third all-time behind two-time NCAA three-mile champion Gerry Lindgren (13:17.0) and Riley (13:35.6).

With a stellar senior year that consisted of his second consecutive cross-country title; undefeated track record; state records in the mile and two-mile; PRs of 1:54.3 in the half-mile and 4:06 in the mile; and the two-mile NR, Prefontaine began to find himself being heavily featured in *Track & Field News* and also listed in the "Faces in the Crowd" section of the June 2, 1969 issue of *Sports Illustrated*, which highlighted the eighteen-year-old's state high school record 880, high school NR two-mile, and state-record mile.

Prefontaine actually extended—and ended—his high school running as a member of the USA National Team, with 5,000-meter races during the summer of 1969 at the U.S.-USSR-British Commonwealth meet in Los Angeles, California, on July 19 (fifth-place 14:40.0); U.S.-Europe meet in Stuttgart, West Germany, on July 31 (third-place 13:52.8); U.S.-West Germany meet in Augsburg, West Germany, on August 5 (second-place 14:07.4); and U.S.-Great Britain meet in London, England, on August 13 (fourth-place 14:38.4).

After high school, his academic and athletic collegiate years were spent at UO from 1969 to 1974. That time frame also included the 1972 U.S. Olympic Track and Field Team Trials at UO, the 1972 Munich Olympic Summer Games in Germany, and many international competitions and trips.

He also often returned home to Coos Bay. One of those times in particular, about six years after he graduated from MHS, was in 1975, when he included his alma mater in the North American series of meets he scheduled for

Marshfield High School track in Coos Bay, Oregon. *Photo by Paul Clerici.*

invited Finnish athletes. As a way to replicate his own experiences competing in Europe and Scandinavia over the years, on May 9 the South Coast International Track Meet was held at MHS between athletes from Finland, Oregon Track Club, Stater Track Club, and UO.

In front of a hometown packed house, Prefontaine won the 2,000 meters in an AR 5:01.4, his last one, which put him at number five all-time. He was celebrated and fêted. And he enjoyed spending time with his fans, friends, and family.

He continued with his tour of Finnish athletes, which concluded three weeks later, on May 29, at the NCAA Preparation Meet at Hayward Field in front of another full house. He ran the meet's final event, the 5,000 meters, in a victorious 13:23.8.

Shortly after the meet, tragically, Prefontaine died in a car accident just outside the UO campus, thirty-nine minutes into May 30, 1975. He was twenty-four years young.

The world was stunned.

After days in a fog, mourners visited Mills-Bryan-Sherwood Funeral Home Chapel in Coos Bay to pay their respects to Prefontaine, who was clad in his Olympic warmup outfit, black Norditalia singlet from Italy that he wore in his last race, and Nike waffle trainer running shoes. On June 2, family, friends, and fans gathered in a moving service at the MHS track on which his legend began only ten years earlier. Prefontaine's father had asked family friend, former UO Duck, and early Nike pioneering employee Geoff Hollister to select the pallbearers; they included track club teammate Jon Anderson, Hollister, childhood friend Jim Seyler, U.S. Olympic teammate and friend Frank Shorter, roommate Bob Williams, and roommate Brent Williams, all attired in track outfits in their friend's honor.

As Prefontaine lay in state in the center of the field toward the west end, the school band played the national anthem. Former coaches Bill Bowerman (UO) and Walt McClure Jr. (MHS) delivered eulogies, both of which were later entered into the public U.S. Congressional Record, due to their historical significance.

"Let us all be grateful that we have been a part of what Steve Prefontaine, the champ, stood for, what he enjoyed, and what he achieved," stated Bowerman. "I first knew Pre through Walt McClure. Pre was fourteen years old. Said Walt, 'Watch this freshman, he's tough and will be a good one.' His desire burned to be the best—and he was. Step by step, as he matured, he reached his goals."

McClure Jr. said, "Greatness is for only a few. The accomplishments of such an individual are often recognized years after the deed, the act. Steve Prefontaine achieved this level during his brief lifetime. He was always in a hurry; his destiny could not allow for a wasted effort."

In addition, there was the reading of a letter written by former UO shotput AAU and NCAA champion Neal Steinhauer, as requested by the Prefontaine family; the singing of an original song performed by its songwriter, East Coast cousin Janine "Jan" Prefontaine; and remarks and Finnish-colored flowers from former UO assistant coach and Finnish long-jumper Rainer Stenius, who remarked, "Steve Prefontaine symbolizes the friendship accumulated with Finnish and British athletes. He allowed us to see America and will forever shine in our hearts."

Prefontaine was laid to rest in a private service at Sunset Memorial Park Cemetery, 63060 Millington Frontage Road, which is situated alongside Oregon Coast Highway Route 101, in Coos Bay. The manicured forty-acre site gently overlooks the Isthmus Slough waterway.

For years, when visitors paid their respects, his flat marble grave marker was usually found by asking for directions and locating the large evergreen shrub behind it. The flat stone featured six lines—"'Pre, Steve R. Prefontaine, 1-25-51 – 5-30-75, Our Beloved Son & Brother Who Raced Through Life

*Top*: Sunset Memorial Park Cemetery in Coos Bay, Oregon. *Photo by Paul Clerici.*

*Bottom*: Early version of Steve Prefontaine grave marker at Sunset Memorial Park Cemetery in Coos Bay, Oregon. *Photos by Paul Clerici.*

Now Rests in Peace"—with a Christian cross at the top left corner and upside-down Olympic rings at the top right.

About twenty-five years later, a vertical upright headstone was installed to be better located by visitors. Along with the new addition of a raised three-quarter profile of Prefontaine's face is the cross, corrected Olympic rings, and the words "'Pre,' Steve R. Prefontaine, Jan. 25, 1951–May 30,

Steve Prefontaine upright headstone at Sunset Memorial Park Cemetery in Coos Bay, Oregon. *Photos by Julie Henning.*

1975, Our beloved son and brother who raced through life now rests in peace." (It is also incumbent upon visitors to remember that this is sacred ground at which to pay respects; more than a usual tourist spot, it should be treated as such.)

Visits to pay respects to Prefontaine have remained consistent over the decades. According to Sunset Memorial Park Cemetery office manager and funeral home and cemetery specialist Diane Morrison-Hille, that was the main reason to improve the visibility of the area.

"I have worked here for twenty-two years," she said in 2022. "After just being here a short time, I realized we get visitors from all over the world. I approached our company about doing an upright so all we have to do is step out the [office] door and point in that direction. The company agreed, and so did his parents. I had the pleasure of designing it. At this time, Pre's mom was pretty blind. I told her when it came in, I would call her to come touch it. I had them make a raised bust of his face (that appears on the upright). The day I called her to come in, I had just the bronze portion so I could lay it down on the counter for her to feel. That day I learned mothers never get over losing one of their children. She laid over on it and just wept. Broke my heart. I believe it was in 2001 or 2002 we did that."

Throughout Coos Bay, Prefontaine had made great use of town roads and land for his training—hill work on Tenth Street; general mileage through the many neighborhoods; hard cardio on sand dunes and beaches along the Siuslaw National Forest region; scenic miles on trails and the expansive landscape of Coos Golf Club, known then as Coos Country Club, at 93884 Coos Sumner Lane; Mingus Park, originally called Marshfield City Park, on land obtained in 1925 and later renamed in honor of Coos Bay Parks Commission chairman Dr. Everett Mingus—some of which help compose the eponymous race course.

He is never far from the thoughts of the people of Coos Bay, whether through precious memories and stories or in an array of heartfelt monuments and memorials.

On the outdoor plaza of the Coos Bay Visitor Information Center at 50 Central Avenue is the Pre Memorial monument that was dedicated five years after his passing, on September 20, 1980, to coincide with the first Prefontaine Memorial Run. Created by UO alumnus Stuart Woods of Coos Bay, it stands approximately nine feet tall, and its three cubic yards of concrete weigh about twelve thousand pounds.

"Aside from the requirements of the bronze plaque—size and security— the monument's design was inspired by the power and stamina of Steve's stride. The base represents the track facilities that he would dominate during his career," Woods explained. "As a neighbor and contemporary growing up in Coos Bay, I watched Steve during his training runs as well as in competition. I attended the University of Oregon during his magical days of impact upon Hayward Field, the entire community, and our country."

Affixed near the top of the concrete torso-style form is a plaque that features a three-quarter relief of Prefontaine's face, dates and locations of his birth and death, and the ARs he held at the time of his passing. (There is also a similar version of this monument in Coos Bay's sister-city of Choshi, Japan. Dedicated in 1986, it stands proudly in Choshi's Central Green Park.)

A few blocks southwest of Coos Bay Visitor Information Center is the Coos Art Museum (CAM), located at 235 Anderson Avenue. In 1985, the Prefontaine Gallery opened to the public on the second floor. Immediately greeting visitors in the CAM lobby is a beautifully colorful Chris Hopkins– created painting of the town legend. And on permanent display in the gallery are running shoes, awards, and other items related to its famous citizen.

"There are quite a few awards, medals, trophies, and pictures," Linda Prefontaine pointed out. "There are around one hundred medals."

As the museum states on its website about the gallery, "On the walls are… photos [that] depict Pre running or crossing the finish line in many of his races, including one from the Olympic Games held in Munich in 1972. Two cases built by Ray Prefontaine are filled with memorabilia of his son's accomplishments, beginning with Pre's days running for Marshfield High

*Above*: Prefontaine Memorial monument in Coos Bay, Oregon. *Photos by Paul Clerici.*

*Right*: Coos Art Museum in Coos Bay, Oregon. *Courtesy Coos Art Museum.*

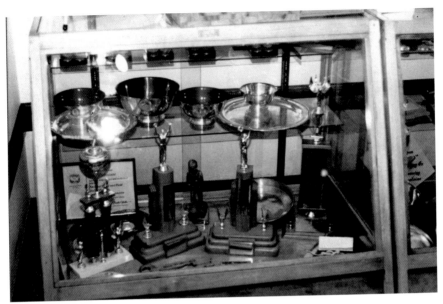

Display case at the Prefontaine Gallery inside Coos Art Museum in Coos Bay, Oregon. *Photo by Paul Clerici.*

School. There are plaques, cups, trophies, and medals on display from his family's collection."

In addition, in the middle of one of the rooms is a large handcrafted wooden conference-size table built by inmates from the Oregon State Penitentiary, at which Prefontaine himself in the early 1970s started a running club for those incarcerated.

Reportedly the only art museum on the Oregon coast, CAM annually welcomes over fourteen thousand patrons from around the world to its refurbished Art Deco 1936 post office building.

"We encourage our visitors to both sign and read through the guest registry. See what those—whom to this day still admire and honor the memory of Steve Prefontaine—have written. Take the time to reflect on the life and career of a young man who influenced so many," the museum states.

While Prefontaine's passing marked the end of an era in terms of his athletic prowess, of course, it did not end his legacy. Over the many decades since, people still recognize Coos Bay and its environs as a true connection to its native son.

In a span of a few years, from 1995 to 1998, major motion pictures and documentaries were made about Prefontaine—*Fire on the Track: The Steve Prefontaine Story*, a one-hour documentary (1995); *Prefontaine* feature film

Prefontaine Gallery display case inside Coos Art Museum in Coos Bay, Oregon. *Photo by Paul Clerici.*

(1997); *Without Limits* feature film (1998)—all of which include Coos Bay, real or replicated.

Just over a quarter-century after his passing, the oval on which he began to shine as a kid was named Steve Prefontaine Track, on April 27, 2001. At a public ceremony attended by family, friends, and fans at the spring Coos County Track Meet, Prefontaine Memorial Committee executive director Bob Huggins served as emcee, with speakers MHS athletic director Tom Jenkins, Linda Prefontaine, Hollister, All-American UO runner Rudy Chapa, MHS state champion Fran Worthen, and Prefontaine teammate and record-setter Jay Farr.

In his public comments to begin the ceremony, Huggins made note of the track itself.

"It was in 1968, Steve Prefontaine's junior year at Marshfield, when a new cinder track was completed. That surface served the school well over the years, but time had taken its toll. This beautiful new track replaces that old cinder surface that had deteriorated badly. The old base had settled and cracked, causing poor drainage. The southwest corner of the track was two feet higher than the northeast corner, causing the short sprint and hurdle races to be run uphill. The old track had non-standard curves, which were too tight, and the lanes were only thirty-six feet wide instead of the standard forty-two-foot lanes," he stated. "What we have ended up with is a high school athletic complex second to none in the state of Oregon that will provide the youth of this community with a state-of-the-art synthetic field and this beautiful track which we are dedicating this evening in the name of Steve Prefontaine."

Through the hindsight of wonderment, Linda Prefontaine with her public comments connected together some of her brother's lifelong accomplishments and honors.

"As children, Steve and I spent countless hours playing on this track and in the old wooden grandstands. Who would have known? As the kid from Coos Bay, he won your hearts. Who would have known? In early June of 1975, we paid tribute to him and memorialized his final lap on this track. Who would have known? The Prefontaine family is proud and honored, as I know Steve truly would be!" she said.

Hollister, who also presented a plaque from Nike that is located at the track, in his public comments mentioned the coaching Prefontaine received that fostered his success.

"I am honored to be here at Marshfield High School to speak on behalf of the two most influential people in my life—Bill Bowerman and Steve Prefontaine. And it is only fitting that their two names be united once more, this time with the dedication of this facility, named in the memory of Steve Prefontaine. Steve was blessed with the mentoring of four fine coaches—at Marshfield, Walt McClure and Phil Pursian; at the University of Oregon, Bill Bowerman and Bill Dellinger. During Bowerman's tenure at Oregon, he coached Walt McClure and Bill Dellinger," Hollister said.

Chapa, who broke Prefontaine's 3,000-meter record in 1979, included in his public comments the attributes that made the honoree the great competitor that he was.

"We are here today to honor Pre, what he accomplished but more importantly what he stood for—drive, vision, determination. That is what really made Pre great, why his spirit still lives. Pre was the greatest athlete ever to come out of Coos Bay, certainly one of the greatest in Oregon history. What made Pre special [wasn't] his great accomplishments, but rather the values he embodied. That's what set him apart," said Chapa.

In Worthen's public comments, she addressed the advocacy of Prefontaine that she admired and from which she benefited.

"Steve Prefontaine was more than a champion on the track. He was a compassionate man, fearless in his outspoken approach to inequity at all levels of college and national sport. He was a champion of women athletes like me who endured discrimination in sports programs at every level but who pressed on for the love of the sport. The torch was not dropped at his untimely death but was passed on to others who drew courage and confidence from Steve's influence in their lives. We have witnessed, and our sons and daughters have benefited from, the changes that have occurred in the twenty-five years since his death," she stated.

In addition to a plaque at the track that recognizes the 2,000-meter AR he set three weeks before his passing—inscribed "Steve Prefontaine set his last American record on this track May 9, 1975, running the 2000m in 5:01.4"—and one that features photos of him running, there also are a number of plaques throughout Coos Bay, from MHS to the town center, and along the course of the Prefontaine Memorial Run.

In 2008, through the Prefontaine Hometown Project, can be found ten plaques of various quotes, including, "The only good race pace is suicide pace, and today looks like a good day to die."; "I'm going to work so that it's a pure guts race at the end, and if it is, I am the only one who can win it."; and "A lot of people run a race to see who is the fastest. I run to see who has the most guts, who can punish himself into exhausting pace, and then at the end, punish himself even more."

At MHS's Pirate Hall, the Prefontaine Memorial Committee dedication plaque, written by member Jay Farr, states, "The most important contribution of our work as individuals who remember Steve, and recall his accomplishments, is to give the youth of our communities the memory of one of our own, which dared to be the best in the world." Below the plaque is a smaller one that includes the most well-known quote by Prefontaine: "To give anything less than your best is to sacrifice the gift."

Some of the plaque locations, which coincide with the race course and local places of interest, include the CAM; Ocean Boulevard; Blossom Gulch Elementary School; and MHS, whose cross-country and track teams are responsible for the semi-annual maintenance and upkeep.

About one mile northeast of MHS and a few blocks southeast from the CAM, on an exterior wall at 275 South Broadway (Route 101) is a stunning thirty-one-foot-high, seventy-foot-wide, full-color, multi-image mural of Prefontaine. There had been plans to produce such an honor for several years. But it finally began in earnest in the spring of 2017, when Erik Nicolaisen of Old City Artists of Portland, Oregon, was contacted. He began submitting proposals to the Coos Bay City Council and Linda Prefontaine for direction, approval, and input, as well as searching for images and selecting partners.

Marshfield High School track in Coos Bay, Oregon. *Photo by Mike Fanelli.*

"The process was pretty fast and furious, but it all came together in the end," Nicolaisen recalled. "Many of the designs, including the final one, were a collaboration with Craig Ferroggiaro at Willamette Valley Color, an amazing Portland photo editor, photographer, and retoucher. Simultaneously I was reaching out to pretty much everyone who may have high-resolution images of Steve Prefontaine, including the estates of several photographers; the *Register-Guard*'s photo editor, Chris Pietsch; the University of Oregon; and Nike, who now owns photographer Rich Clarkson's voluminous Prefontaine archive. They were all gracious enough to either locate original photographs that I was looking for or allow me to sift through their archives in search of photos."

The final selection is a combination of images that represent a cross-section of Prefontaine's competitive career, which spans from high school to UO and the Olympics.

"This final design was one of the most simple, and least busy, of the submitted designs—but it was a stunner," Nicolaisen pointed out. "It would highlight Pre in iconic periods of his life. The first was a photo of Pre in his high school days in front of the old bleachers at Marshfield High School that had since burned down; the Pre picture was an old one from a state meet in Eugene that we combined with an archival photo of the Marshfield bleachers and track. The one in the middle was a shot of Pre hitting that final turn in a race in college. The last was a picture of him representing the

USA in the Olympics. The city, Linda, and myself all agreed that this mural design would be unmissable from the main highway and would continue to quickly tell the story of the local boy who rose to amazing heights."

The process by which to correctly replicate a recognizable real-life subject on such a large scale, and on the less-than-ideal canvas of an exterior wall exposed to harsh Oregon weather, is both simple and complex.

"We employ pretty much the same process that Michelangelo used to paint the Sistine Chapel. We fabricate a crude template, or 'pattern,' that once laid out, ensures that things are scaled correctly and reside where they need to be on the wall," Nicolaisen described. "We pre-mix a palate of oil paints for the artwork, then we ultimately depend on the amazing talent of our artists. Large-scale murals in general require serious talent, but a permanent and unmistakable portraits of the town's golden boy has very little margin for error. All credit is due to our team accurately nailing these likenesses."

Progression of Steve Prefontaine mural in Coos Bay, Oregon, by Old City Artists. *Courtesy Old City Artists.*

Beachfront where Steve Prefontaine often trained in Coos Bay, Oregon. *Photo by Linda Prefontaine/Prefontaine Productions LLC.*

While seemingly complete as it currently appears, Nicolaisen reveals there is an additional element that may still be included in the future, something he has always envisioned.

"I really wanted for the center picture to employ a trompe-l'oeil technique, with an actual running track continuing from the wall and onto the actual ground of that space, turning and going down the corridor. It would allow the mural to interact with visitors even more, and it really fit for the shape of this space," he explained. "Unfortunately, there was just no time to get this done in 2017. There has been some discussion of the possibility of including this down the line."

For Nicolaisen personally, the subject matter and the project itself resonated with special meaning.

"As an Oregonian and an ex–University of Oregon athlete, I was well aware of Pre's inspirational story, and throughout my athletic career I was regularly inspired with Pre's quotes by my coaches," he said. "So to get to travel to Pre's hometown, work closely with his little sister, and meet his friends and teammates was all a very special treat. The magnitude of the final mural was not lost on me. I am so honored to have been a part of creating a lasting tribute to Steve and his legacy."

As interest in Prefontaine continued—and continues—people visit his hometown in search of related places and sites where they can find a connection to him.

Shortly after Linda Prefontaine returned to Coos Bay from residing in Eugene for years, she created the Tour de Pre, which has organically grown to an engaging, entertaining, informative, and caring guide to her brother's life and their hometown.

"Currently, it's a seven-hour private tour," she said of the personalized trips, bookings of which began in 2017. "This is a unique and one-of-a-kind tour. No one else can duplicate or even come close to reproducing this tour."

In addition to hearing stories from her and visiting the many sites of Coos Bay, people can also run laps on Steve Prefontaine Track at MHS and even attempt the sand dunes on which he trained along the Oregon Dunes National Recreation Area and beaches on which he practiced at Horsfall Beach.

"Linda Prefontaine is really the steward of Steve's flame," noted Nicolaisen. "She is so sweet and knowledgeable and so selflessly committed to furthering her brother's legacy. Her personal tour of Steve's local spots and museum in Coos Bay—the Tour de Pre—is such a cool sightseeing opportunity for any Prefontaine fans who make it to his hometown. The mural is one of the stops. I highly recommend it."

# Chapter 3

# EUGENE, UNIVERSITY OF OREGON, GLENWOOD, SALEM...

About one hundred miles northeast of Steve Prefontaine's hometown of Coos Bay is the city of Eugene, in Lane County, Oregon. It was named after mid-nineteenth-century settler and Illinois county sheriff Eugene Franklin Skinner, who with his wife, Mary Cook Skinner, and others, explored the Native American Kalapuyan (Confederated Tribes of the Grand Ronde/Siletz) land along Willamette Valley. Founded in 1846, the eventual forty-four-square-mile parcel was once known as Eugene City. Incorporated in 1862, it became Eugene in 1889.

The Eugene area is where Prefontaine spent the majority of his adult life, from ages eighteen to twenty-four, in places such as Glenwood, Salem, and Eugene itself at residences and the University of Oregon (UO).

Located on 295 acres at 1585 East 13th Street, UO was born in 1859 when the U.S. Congress "required the founders of Oregon to establish a university," which it did when UO opened in 1876.

Former UO Duck Parker Stinson—who competed at Hayward Field as a twelve-year-old 3,000-meter third-place finisher at the 2004 USATF National Junior Olympic Track and Field Championships, as a high school three-time U.S. Junior Champion 10K winner, and as a nine-time All-American—lovingly described the campus.

"It's so green and lush and beautiful. It's so earthy; nature and natural; clean—it just felt like the university and the track and nature and everything all kind of molded together," he said. "And there's Hendricks Park, where I'd go run a lot up in these beautiful hills and trees, and it's right there! You're

University of Oregon. *Photo by Paul Clerici.*

in the hustle and bustle of campus, and all of a sudden you feel like you're in the middle of nowhere on a run. It was awesome! I felt welcome there."

According to the UO Office of the Registrar, Prefontaine enrolled for the fall term on September 20, 1969. He majored in speech: broadcast communication, and his bachelor of science degree was conferred on June 9, 1974.

As an underclassman, Prefontaine lived in a few places, among them Douglass Hall, in the south wing of UO's Walton Complex, 1595 East 15th Street (in 2013, at the other end of the block, a five-story, twenty-unit student residence named The Prefontaine was built at 1801 University Street, at the corner of 18th Avenue); the Pi Kappa Alpha's UO Gamma Pi fraternity house ΠΚΑ at 1414 Alder Street in Eugene, a few blocks from UO; and a duplex.

Gamma Pi chapter president and recruiting/rush director John Kaegi, a junior at the time, brought in Prefontaine by way of a Coos Bay schoolmate from Marshfield High School (MHS) who had joined earlier in the fall of 1968.

"We hung out for the week. Having made friends with him and gained his trust, we invited him to skip all the BS of rush week at Oregon and just join ΠΚΑ, which he did," said Kaegi, who had made the recruiting trip to Coos Bay in August 1969. "He was part of a huge pledge class that was announced in late September 1969 of around twenty-eight to thirty freshmen, so Steve was initiated sometime around April of 1970. It was the custom for fall pledges to be initiated into full membership in the spring term. The old days of fraternity rites of passage and hazing were long gone at Oregon in those days, replaced with requirements to learn about the history—dating back to 1868—and policies of the fraternity, learn everyone's name and background, and make grades. He accomplished all of that and successfully navigated his initiatory week, including tests for fraternity and member knowledge and 'sensitivity' training focused on understanding and adopting brotherhood-building skills."

Prefontaine also had the chance to visit the fraternity earlier than most pledges.

"He was the first freshman of his class to be offered membership as a pledge, which occurred before school even started. I don't recall whether that broke some kind of rush rule at the time," Kaegi noted. "He accepted once he saw the house and met the guys, well before any of the other freshmen visited the house during rush week. He was the only varsity athlete."

There was an "understanding" that UO coach Bill Bowerman's runners were heavily discouraged from joining fraternities.

"Coach Bill Bowerman refused to allow track and field athletes to live in fraternities, until Prefontaine challenged him and became the first. I never found out how he was able to move out of the dorm and into the house in spring term. Back then, residential freshmen were not permitted to live outside the dorm unless they were Eugene natives," recalled Kaegi. "I believe he not only persuaded Bowerman to allow him to live in the fraternity house, where he was the breakfast cook to earn a little extra money, but he got Bowerman to pull strings somehow. Steve lived in a jock dorm his first two terms at Oregon, but he began to see the members of Gamma Pi also as his friends. So he spent most of his time at the fraternity house, using my room or the library to study or to entertain his dates or to shoot the bull with members."

Kaegi feels that Prefontaine felt comfortable with the fraternity brothers and also enjoyed the house itself.

"Trusting people was difficult for Steve. By the time he arrived at Oregon, having just turned eighteen, he had already been let down by people he trusted many times," said Kaegi. "He trusted us. And he enjoyed the facility itself, which was more modern, for the time, than the classic fraternity houses around campus. It featured a sunken living room with a big stereo/radio that was always playing music and a large dining room and a game

Steve Prefontaine's Pi Kappa Alpha Gammi Pi fraternity house in Eugene, Oregon. *Courtesy Pi Kappa Alpha Fraternity.*

room with pool and Foosball tables, etc., and TVs. Pledging Prefontaine really upset [the Alpha Sigma chapter of] Theta Chi—which, by the way, was actually my original fraternity legacy at UO—where most of the track athletes were members."

By Prefontaine's 1971-72 junior year, UO's Gamma Pi chapter was facing possible closure, as frat life was losing its popularity in some areas of the country. Campus life in parts of America was growing volatile; demonstrations against the Vietnam War were occurring nationwide; and there was concern about the status of student draft deferments (which ended in 1971) and the Selective Service System lottery during the war years.

The actual fraternity building in which Prefontaine lived was the third Gamma Pi house and was built in 1962. But when the 1931 local chapter charter was canceled after forty-one years, the house was eventually sold in 1976.

"He was an active member of ΠΚΑ throughout his first three years of college, until the chapter charter was withdrawn in 1972 for its inability to cover house mortgage payments," Kaegi explained. "He and I were members through the most intense anti-fraternity years in campus history. By 1970, almost no one wanted to live in a fraternity house. The ΠΚΑ headquarters pulled the charter when it was obvious that members could no longer keep up with mortgage payments and monthly membership fees."

Even during and after the demise of Gamma Pi at UO, Kaegi recalled Prefontaine's continued support for the fraternity and his brothers.

"In 1974, when the anti-fraternity movement had cooled and another house was found a stone's throw away [in Oregon], I returned to the campus with one of our chapter consultants to endeavor to restart and recharter the chapter," said Kaegi, at the time the national headquarters director of communications. "The first person I called on was Steve and asked him to participate in the effort. He enthusiastically agreed to give as much time as he could, considering his training schedule. He came to several introductory parties, which of course drew lots of guys from the dorms who hadn't yet committed to a fraternity but who wanted to meet him. He helped us reestablish the group with about twenty-four or so new pledges and was still meeting with them through the spring of 1975 until he passed away." (Gamma Pi chapter in Oregon was rechartered in 1977.)

Entering his junior year at UO, Prefontaine bought a thirty-six-foot single-wide trailer in which he resided for two years, from 1972 to 1973. Located at Riverbank Trailer Park on Franklin Boulevard in Glenwood, an "unincorporated community" town along the Willamette River near Springfield, it was less than three miles east of UO. Fellow Duck teammate Pat Tyson once again became his roommate.

"He called me over to the trailer for dinner and said, 'How'd you like to room with me?' He and his girlfriend asked me. And I said okay," Tyson recalls. "I thought maybe I made a bad choice of leaving my old roommate—we had a lease on an apartment—but how do you say no to Pre? And I was not afraid of living with him either; some people might think it might be almost too much. But I looked at it as he was going to give me a lot of stuff that'll make me better."

In addition to securing some privacy, since it was off-campus housing, the purchase also was economical.

"He *bought* it, so it was *his* trailer, and he wasn't throwing away rent because it was his. The rental space was like $25 a month. Propane is what heated it, and it was $7.50 a month. We did our own laundry at the laundry shack at the trailer park. He was very proud of it. It was clean," noted Tyson. "We were right next to the railroad tracks, which was pretty crazy. It took a little while to get used to the trailer jumping around when the train went by. But you got used to it, and after a while you're fine. And there was a neighbor and his wife—they were like Hells Angels on bikes—that worked at a charcoal barbecue briquet place, and they'd invite us over for barbecues. The people he loved being around were the simple blue-collar people. That's why he lived in the trailer park. It was something out of *The Grapes of Wrath*. He loved that trailer!"

Those years at Glenwood also were some of Prefontaine's most fruitful and busy in terms of competitions and commitments, which included among them the Olympic Trials at UO, Olympic Games at Munich, and his red-shirted cross-country season.

"There's no way you're going to run cross-country after a long, long track season. He did run the spring of '73 that same academic year and then came back the fall of '73 to run that cross-country wearing the Oregon [school] jersey and won [the 1973 NCAA title] in Spokane, Washington, against Nick Rose. In the fall of '73, he ran cross-country and then graduated," noted Tyson. "He went four and one-third years; we were on the quarter system back then." (UO's academic quarter system consists of four terms, with the academic year at the time beginning with the summer term: July-August summer term, September-December fall term, January-March winter term, April-June spring term.)

Around this time, Prefontaine also tended bar at the Paddock Saloon and Grill Tavern at 3355 East Amazon Drive (to where it moved in 1964), about two miles south of UO. While "The Pad" differs from that time, his image nevertheless adorns the menu, glasses, and walls.

"He loved the freedom of getting in the car or going into a bar and meeting people or going to the Paddock, where there was a woman working there, and she'd make these big burgers and fries, and he would give her a big smooch and she loved it!" Tyson recalled. "And he'd walk around and say hello to everybody and maybe play a game of Frogger or air hockey or Foosball or pool and just engage with everybody. He was the life of the party."

But, as Tyson also explained, Prefontaine wasn't always the human magnet or the athletic-hyped "Pre" who people saw in the newsreels and self-induced pre-race fanfare.

"At the trailer, he might be sitting down writing letters and answering the phone all at the same time. I don't like to use the word seriousness…it was just where we lived, and we ate and we chatted some, and then maybe his girlfriend would be over," Tyson described. "He was always the life of the party and he liked to socialize—that's just who he was. The only way he wouldn't be [that 'life of the party'] was when he was back in the trailer and was chillin'. Why would he have to be the center of attention with me? Now, he *was* the life of the party and he *did* love to socialize. But when he was at home in the trailer or in an academic classroom where he's going to be the student, he's not the center of attention."

However, Tyson quickly added, "On the other hand, when you're driving around in an MG and the top's down with a hot blonde in the car, everybody on campus is looking and saying, 'Oh, there's Steve!' A lot of people looked at him wrongly. I think a lot of people looked at him as cocky and in love with himself. He could come across that way, but they just didn't know who he was. One time, I was hitchhiking home up in Seattle, and I had a guy stop in a pickup truck and the radio was on, and it was talking about Steve Prefontaine. I didn't tell him he was my roommate, and he starts, 'Ah, that bastard, that son-of-a-bitch, he's so cocky.' I laughed and said, 'Yup, he probably is.' There was that perception by a lot of people, too."

In July 1972, Prefontaine qualified for the 5,000 meters at the U.S. Olympic Track and Field Team Trials at UO, and two months later, he finished fourth in that event at the 1972 Munich Olympic Summer Games.

Shortly after the Olympics, he returned home to his trailer to resume his studies at UO. He did train—and on occasion run the Laurelwood Golf Course at 2700 Columbia Street in Eugene—with and without his fellow Ducks because of his eligibility for 1973 cross-country.

Prefontaine's coaching changed in 1972-73 when Bowerman first reduced his daily coaching in 1972 and then officially retired in 1973, in part to help with UO's fundraising need to replace and restore aging sections of Hayward Field.

In his twenty-four-year Hall of Fame coaching career, Bowerman amassed a 114-20 dual-meet record, 10 undefeated seasons, 4 NCAA team titles, 24 NCAA individual titles, 38 conference winners, 64 All-Americans, 33 Olympians, and was a U.S. Olympic Team assistant coach at the 1968 Mexico Summer Games and U.S. Olympic Team head coach at the 1972 Munich Summer Games.

Taking over was Bill Dellinger, a three-time All-American Duck, five-year UO assistant coach, three-time U.S. Olympian, and 1964 Tokyo Olympic Summer Games 5,000-meter bronze medalist. And he had already been working closely with Prefontaine.

Between indoors and outdoors, in the spring of 1974, Prefontaine moved from his trailer to a house on Amazon Drive in Eugene and then about five miles away to a house on McKinley Street, still in Eugene.

He also joined the local Oregon Track Club (OTC). One of the events the group organized was the OTC International-Style Cross-Country races (5K, 6K, 12K) at Lane Community College, 4000 East 30th Avenue, in Eugene,

University of Oregon coach Bill Bowerman statue at Historic Hayward Field. *Photos by Paul Clerici.*

on September 28, 1974. In a time of 37:37, Prefontaine won the 12K (7.45 miles), the course of which featured "a deep ditch to climb, hills to storm, a water jump to cross, and steeplechase barriers to hurdle," as detailed in the OTC newsletter.

Athletically, his head was focused on the 1976 U.S. Olympic Track and Field Team Trials, to be held at UO in June 1976; and subsequent Games of the XXI Olympiad, in Montreal, Canada.

Part of the buildup was a series of meets between American athletes and Finnish athletes, three of which he organized in May 1975 for Oregon (Madras, Coos Bay, Eugene), Canada (Burnaby), and California (Modesto).

After Pre won the Oregon Twilight Meet 10,000 meters (28:09.4) on April 26, the first Finnish Tour Meet event was held at Madras High School in Madras, Oregon, where he won the 3,000 meters in 8:26.4. He followed that with his last AR, fittingly on his high school track at MHS in Coos Bay, with a 5:01.4 in the 2,000 meters. The third stop was at the British Columbia International Meet in Burnaby, British Columbia, Canada, where he won the 5,000 meters in 13:46.8. Nine days later was the 1975 California Relays at Modesto Junior College in Modesto, California, where he won the two-mile in 8:36.4.

And in the final U.S.-Finland matchup, on May 29, at Hayward Field in the NCAA Preparation Meet, he won the 5,000 meters in 13:23.8—over 1972 U.S. Olympic Marathon gold medalist Frank Shorter—in what turned out to be Prefontaine's final competition.

Various published public reports and interviews detail that Prefontaine lingered a bit afterward with fans, friends, and family at Hayward Field. Then, in his favorite bronze yellow 1973 MGB (Morris Garage model B) four-speed manual two-door roadster sportscar, he reportedly made his way to the Walnut Street apartment of friends and fellow Ducks Steve Bence and Mark Feig, ten blocks east, to clean up. He then stopped by the UO track and field awards banquet at the Black Angus Restaurant at 2123 Franklin Boulevard in Eugene and there with Dellinger discussed some training. Prefontaine reportedly followed that with a brief stop at the Paddock with his girlfriend before they joined the post-meet party at friend and former Duck Geoff Hollister's house on Dillard Road, where friends, family, and fellow athletes were celebrating.

Shorter, who was staying at former Duck Kenny Moore's house on Prospect Drive, left the gathering with Prefontaine. According to Shorter, "We went to Geoff Hollister's house for the party and had a few beers there and we left early. He took his girlfriend—she was in the car—took her to her car, and he drove me back to Kenny's, and we sat out front talking about where we were going to go from there with regard to the professionalism and trying to earn prize money. We talked for two minutes or so and agreed to meet for a ten-mile run the next morning. And he drove around the corner and a minute later he was…gone. Less than two minutes."

Prospect Drive—about a mile and a half east of Hayward Field and approximately four and half miles from Prefontaine's house on McKinley Street—is situated just around the corner from Skyline Boulevard, where the accident occurred.

Shorter, who says he did not hear the accident, describes, "It just happened. It was one of those sort of perfect storm, perfect incidents. He got driven off the road.…The MGB had a rollbar, and there was a retaining wall, and on [one] side just mountain and no room. Except at one spot where's this big bunker and then more of a retaining wall. He was driven off the road, and he hit the boulder. The car went over on the rollbar, and he wasn't wearing a seatbelt, and he was pinned by the car and he suffocated. He died of suffocation. So…that was…it."

According to the official Oregon Police Department report, Prefontaine drove down Skyline Boulevard, headed toward Birch Lane. At the

Pre's Rock, white area in center, at Skyline Boulevard in Eugene, Oregon. *Photo by Paul Clerici.*

penultimate curve on Skyline, he veered across the center of the road onto the facing northbound lane. Officer-observed on-road scuff marks, left by rotating front tires sliding sideways, gave indication that the car skidded to the side of the road, where it jumped the curb, traveled about four feet in the dirt, and hit a vertical rock embankment. The angle and force of impact caused the open-top convertible to flip over onto its rollbar top. Prefontaine, the police observed on arrival, did not have his seatbelt on, and the car had landed on top of him, on Skyline, about 150 feet west of Birch. Neighbors who heard the noise on the quiet street, shortly after midnight, responded to the accident and called police. On their arrival, police found Prefontaine dead at the scene from "traumatic asphyxiation." The time of the accident is listed as 12:39 a.m. Friday morning, about four hours after he finished his final race. He was twenty-four.

Within hours, by daybreak, word of the tragedy had begun to quickly spread.

"For most of us on the team and [who were] friends with Pre, Pre's death was our first death experience with a close friend," recalled Bence, who had competed in the NCAA Prep, which Moore and a *Sports Illustrated* photographer covered for the magazine.

Skyline Boulevard in Eugene, Oregon, with Pre's Rock on the right. *Photo by Paul Clerici.*

Bence had also enjoyed the hours before the meet with Prefontaine and friends, playing cards at his house while relaxing beforehand.

"For me," he said, "it was very surreal that I spent Thursday with Pre, raced with him on that day, had several pictures taken with him, and he vowed to be my new coach starting on Saturday."

Tyson, who was home in Seattle, Washington, where he taught and coached, and had a race the same night as the NCAA Prep, had already planned to travel to Eugene the day Prefontaine died.

"I remember going up[stairs] and shaving, and I cut myself, and there was a little bit of blood dripping and I said, 'I guess I'm not dreaming.' It was just disbelief," he recalled. "Very warm, sunny, bright late May Friday morning, and I got in my car and drove up to my school I was working at, and the kids there had heard about it on the news. And here we are five hours from Eugene; we're in Seattle! But he was a guest at our school, so everybody, including the principal, they all came into my room and consoled me, and they knew I was going to be going to Eugene that afternoon anyway."

On his way to Eugene—with a college student he was bringing home to Oregon—Tyson's thoughts were racing to catch up.

"As we drove down the highway—I-5, about a five-hour drive—every radio station had it," Tyson remembered of the trip. "You crossed the

Columbia River in Portland and it seemed to be more intense and more detailed messages about it. And then Eugene."

Once he arrived in Eugene, Tyson made his way to Prefontaine's McKinley Street house to meet up with friends for consolation and comfort. And as with most who still doubted the veracity of the news, a sense of closure propelled some to Skyline.

"When I got to Eugene, the first thing I did was I went over to Pre's house and saw some of his roommates, and we were all in shock. Then I went up to where the accident was, just to make sure," he says. "There was some oil and little debris from the car. This was less than twenty-four hours after he died, and it was like verifying that he is dead, but you just don't want to believe it; that's why you go there, to prove that this is wrong. It was just numbing; thinking no way Pre's going to be gone because Pre was the glue that kept all of us together, just like a relative in some families have that person that was the glue. I think we're pretty tight in the runners' world because of Pre. Even though we don't all know each other, we know each other through Pre—brothers and sisters for good."

The fragility of life struck many that day. U.S. Olympian Marty Liquori, the third U.S. high school athlete to run a sub-4:00 mile and who also competed against Prefontaine, recognized the suddenness of mortality on which most people that age don't focus.

Steve Prefontaine Memorial, also known as Pre's Rock, on Skyline Boulevard in Eugene, Oregon. *Photo by Julie Henning.*

"His death greatly impacted the sport in the sense that many of us tried very hard and made sacrifices, thinking that our lives would be better after we retired," noted Liquori, a chronic lymphocytic leukemia survivor since the 1990s. "When Pre died, we realized nothing is guaranteed in this life, and I think a lot of us started to enjoy life more. And those of us who were older perhaps did not sacrifice as much as we had in our younger careers. So in that way, I think he had a great impact on the sport."

The day after Prefontaine's passing, a young neighbor reportedly drew in white paint "5-30-75 R.I.P." on a flat surface of the rock embankment. The previously nondescript area soon became a memorial touching point where people came to pay their respects and express their emotions.

An outpouring of grief and support came from all walks of life, from young kids to senior citizens, budding athletes to Olympic legends, the mayor of Eugene to the president of the United States. In a June 5, 1975 letter mailed to Prefontaine's parents and obtained through the Gerald R. Ford Presidential Library, U.S. President Gerald R. Ford wrote, in part, "Mrs. Ford and I were deeply saddened to learn of the tragic accident which took the life of your son, Steve, and we want you to know that you are very much in our thoughts and prayers at this time. We hope the knowledge that your sorrow and sense of loss is shared by your fellow citizens will serve to comfort you in the days ahead. Mrs. Ford joins me in extending our deepest sympathy to you and your family."

Services included his funeral at MHS and burial at Sunset Memorial Park Cemetery in Coos Bay on June 2, followed the next day by a memorial service at Hayward Field. Combined speakers included Bowerman, former MHS coach Walt McClure Jr., Moore, and Shorter.

At the June 6, 1975 U.S. Congressional public session of the U.S. Senate, U.S. Senator Henry M. Jackson of Washington mentioned the passing of Prefontaine. U.S. Senator Mark Hatfield of Oregon, who had issued remarks and condolences when Prefontaine died, said he delayed further reflection until after he could collect additional tributes and stories to be included in the public U.S. Congressional Record, which he did at the July 10, 1975 U.S. Congressional session.

"Pre was an Oregon tiger in the finest tradition—fiercely competitive, confident, and outgoing," stated Senator Hatfield. "As a track fan, I have helped officiate at various meets in Eugene, and I know the unique spirit that fills the University of Oregon track stadium, Hayward Field. The last time that I helped officiate in Eugene was during the 1972 Olympic Trials, and the atmosphere was alive with emotions, not only from the

University of Oregon student residence The Prefontaine. *Photo by Erik Bishoff.*

athletes themselves, as one might expect, but from the supercharged track audience."

With heavy hearts, on June 9, a five-mile Steve Prefontaine Memorial Run was held by the OTC at Alton Baker Park, along the north-bank side of Willamette River, in Eugene. Hollister was the race director, and funds were donated to the newly created Steve Prefontaine Foundation.

Also at the four-hundred-acre Alton Baker Park—named after former *Register Guard* newspaper publisher and owner Alton F. Baker Sr., whose interest in area parkland helped develop this acreage—Prefontaine's early vision of a European/Scandinavian-style running trail became reality.

"Pre loved the running trails in Europe, in particular Finland. I think there were miles of cross-country skiing trails in Finland, which became long running trails in the summer," Bence pointed out. "I heard that Pre drew up some concepts in his notebook of what the running trails could look like in Eugene."

As early as August 1975, organized plans for Prefontaine's Running Trail (Pre's Trail) were being cemented, so to speak, headed by OTC's Ray Hendrickson and Dr. Bill McHolick. A trail of woodchips and sawdust was laid out in time for a dedication event on Labor Day Monday, September 1, 1975. Nearly five hundred runners participated in open and high school races of 3,000 meters, 5,000 meters, and 10,000 meters.

*Opposite, top*: Pre's Trail near University of Oregon's Autzen Stadium in Eugene, Oregon. *Photo by Vern Rogers.*

*Opposite, bottom*: Pre's Trail sign in December 1977 with Greater Boston Track Club runner Bob Hodge, *left*, and Ron Durand. *Courtesy Bob Hodge.*

*Above*: Pre's Trail in Eugene, Oregon. *Photo by Vern Rogers.*

Over the years, there have been many additions and improvements, including lights; surfaces (soft bark, dirt, gravel, woodchips, asphalt); connecting it to the Willamette River Trail; additional loops of varying distances; and other upgrades and restorations. Pre's Trail is located off Martin Luther King Jr. Boulevard and can also be accessed from UO via Frohnmayer Footbridge and Knickerbocker Footbridge.

About three miles southeast of Pre's Trail, back on the other side of the Willamette River, is the 1.5-acre site where Prefontaine died on Skyline Boulevard. The rock embankment, which became known colloquially as Pre's Rock, quickly became a place where people visited to pay their respects and leave items and objects of meaning, including race bib numbers, running shoes, loved ones' ashes, medals, and photos, among them. A pilgrimage for some, its location so close to UO provides a stream of people on some occasions.

According to City of Eugene Public Works Parks and Open Space Planning principal landscape architect Emily Proudfoot, the land area—officially known as the Steve Prefontaine Memorial—has changed ownership since the accident.

"The property was originally owned by the Oregon Department of Transportation [ODOT], and when it came up for sale, the City didn't have the needed funds for acquiring the property. There was enough community interest, however, that [Nike co-founder and former Duck] Phil Knight agreed to reimburse the City for the purchase price. This came with several contractual stipulations that are detailed in the deed of sale," she explained. "The City of Eugene Parks is responsible for upkeep of the land. We provide very minimal maintenance in the area, outside of trash pickup and occasional checking in on the site, but we've taken care to preserve and protect [the black stone marker] through recent site safety updates."

In 1994, about twenty years after his passing, a miniature statue of Prefontaine suddenly appeared on that rock embankment. Affixed to its façade, the small three-dimensional running form seemed to emerge from the stone itself one day. Prior to that, it was only the cold, hard wall of rock that greeted visitors.

Eugene runner John Miller came up with the idea and made a figure in sculpture art class while he attended Lane Community College and kept it at home for years. Later, he sculpted a second figure; while similar to the first, it was more suited for his plan.

Miller's longtime friend Tim Lewis remembered:

"The bronze statue of Pre was all John Miller. He created the statue soon after Pre's death," Lewis said. "I was living with John in the early '90s and that's when he hatched the idea of attaching it to the rock. The statue is around eight to ten inches tall. Pre is wearing an Oregon singlet and a mustache. Pre's stride and his cocked head to one side is perfectly re-created by John. The statue is created out of bronze, which will last longer than the rock it's attached to."

Miller drilled two holes into the rock as phase one. Later, with Lewis, and no fanfare or announcement, they affixed the statue to the rock.

"I was with John when we attached Pre to his rock. I was on lookout as he epoxied Pre," Lewis explained. "John welded two bronze posts to the back of the statue, and then in the middle of the night he drilled two holes into the

Steve Prefontaine statue attached to Pre's Rock. *Photo by Julie Henning.*

rock, and the following day he put epoxy within the holes and then inserted Pre onto Pre's Rock. Once done, we drank a six-pack of Rolling Rock beer along with Pre, pouring a few ounces on the rock. We never told anyone and would go back every now and then and drink a few Rolling Rocks and talk about old times." (The identity of the creator remained largely a secret until Lewis passed away, and Miller endeavors to have his friend remembered.)

A few years later, in 1997, a polished black granite stone marker, adorned with the iconic Brian Lanker "penetrating stare" image of Prefontaine, joined Pre's Rock. It was created by inmates at Oregon State Penitentiary (OSP).

In one of Prefontaine's classes while at UO, the students paid a visit to Oregon's maximum-security prison. Located in the state capital of Salem, OSP houses approximately 2,200 inmates, from minimum to maximum levels of security, including death row; but about 90 percent are released back into society, according to OSP.

The time spent with the inmates resonated with the underclassman, who subsequently on several occasions returned to OSP to help coach, train, and run with those incarcerated. The result was the formation of a running program inside the walls. Very few outside OSP at the time knew of Prefontaine's benevolence.

The running program became the Oregon State Penitentiary Athletic Club (OSPAC). According to OSP, "The Athletic Club started in 1970. The club consists of five inmate executive-body members—president, vice president, treasurer, secretary, and meeting facilitator—and consists of up to 150 inmate club members. To join the Athletic Club, an inmate must have at least one year [of] clear conduct. The Athletic Club is very popular and has a waiting list of 50 or more inmates."

For decades, even for inmates who never met Prefontaine, the OSPAC has remained a successful program with myriad benefits.

"I have a theory, but of course, I am no expert, just my opinion," surmised OSPAC staff advisor Bill Marion, "but some of these guys have addictive behaviors and if you can get them involved in something positive, it can change their lives and keep them out of trouble. Some of them replace drugs, etc., with running. Also, as far their attitude goes, it's really hard to tell what is happening because they have to be Level 3 to join; Level 3 are guys that have been out of trouble for a year or more. It's also very similar to human nature, high school kids, etc.—keep them busy physically and it will improve their lives."

When Prefontaine died, those inside OSP were also affected.

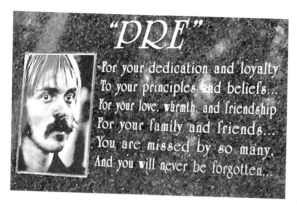

"PRE"

For your dedication and loyalty
To your principles and beliefs...
For your love, warmth, and friendship
For your family and friends...
You are missed by so many.
And you will never be forgotten...

Pre's Rock monument stone made by Oregon State Penitentiary inmates in honor of Steve Prefontaine. *Photo by Julie Henning.*

"He meant so much to the running program and to the inmates here at OSP that in 1997 the inmates raised funds for a mounting stone and penned those words on the iconic headstone which, ever since, has marked the curve on Skyline Boulevard in Eugene where he died," according to OSP about the etched passage: "For your dedication and loyalty; To your principles and beliefs; For your love, warmth, and friendship; For your family and friends; You are missed by so many; And you will never be forgotten."

With the help of such legendary coaches as Dellinger and Athletics West's Dick Brown, the program continued at OSP.

"Many runners and coaches have kept the program alive to show inmates everything running can offer—rehabilitation, fulfillment, connection, mental and emotional escape," stated OSP.

The OSPAC has grown to feature within the 26-foot walls several races— 5K, 10K, half-marathon—of multiple laps on a 2,250-foot loop, from the spring to the fall. Races include the participation of "guest" runners from the outside, whose interaction also helps those inmates who will eventually be released back into society.

"[Non-inmates] don't or can't comprehend how very important it is for these guys to have outside interaction with our guest runners," Marion noted. "For some of these guys, having an outside person run with them makes them feel human and feel free for a few minutes. Once everything has been taken away from them and they are in prison, their self-worth is so low, and some of them actually have a conscience and feel bad for what they did. I am not speaking for all of them, but there is a percentage of them that want to do better. Running takes them away from these thoughts and releases natural hormones that boost their mental well-being. There again, I am not an expert, but it's pretty well proven and documented these things are true."

Steve Brown, whose father, Dick Brown, helped coach after Dellinger, recalled the impact the running program had on many inmates. "[One inmate] was undefeated for five years in prison races and has since run in the Boston and New York City Marathons. I believe he now works as a rehab counselor. When our dad passed away, [he] attended the memorial service and spoke about his relationship with our dad," he remembered.

It's the long-lasting effect that Brown sees as beneficial, and not just with the inmates.

"I think that most people probably go into a race thinking it will be a one-time event for them. That they will get a nice story to share at parties," he said. "But for a few—and this applies to my dad and to some extent to me—the experience opens them to the humanity of the inmates, to their struggles to become better people; not just healthier, but better. And this is a struggle we all have. So when that connection is made, those people come back and run again, or coach, and invite others, some of whom also feel that connection and choose to engage more deeply."

UO athletic department's Steve DiNatale, who in 2004 with his wife ran a 10K inside OSP, felt comfortable running alongside the inmates.

"They did background tests on all of us," explained DiNatale. "We went to the front desk, signed a waiver that stated they do not negotiate if we are taken hostage, then we were searched and put through an X-ray machine. We went through a door which was locked behind us before they opened the next door ahead of us. I think we went through three or four doors until we were into the main yard where the track was. We were told to stay together until the race started. We were encouraged to talk with the inmates and give them support. Once the race started, we were on our own. Many guards were present, including a guard in each of the towers with long guns. I felt fine amongst the inmates. After the race, we hung out for a while and that was it. I would do it again and would encourage others to do so also. The guys really look forward to having runners from the outside to run with."

The black stone marker by OSP inmates was reportedly given to the ODOT. After languishing in inventory limbo, it was eventually reportedly purchased and donated by Knight and installed at Pre's Rock in 1997.

In 2022, six months before the World Athletics Championship at UO, the first major landscaping project at Pre's Rock finished to improve the safety of those who visit the area.

"The Prefontaine Memorial site has *a lot* of community interest for a ton of different reasons," noted Proudfoot. "After the purchase of the property, the City did add some parking bays just uphill of the site for visitor parking.

*Above*: Steve Prefontaine Memorial (Pre's Rock) with safety improvements made in 2022. *Courtesy City of Eugene.*

*Left*: Track Town USA in Eugene, Oregon. *Courtesy Bill Squires.*

[In 2022,] we were able to add a four-foot-wide sidewalk and small viewing area that is dedicated to park visitation and keeps visitors out of the travel lanes of traffic on the blind corner. We adjusted the siting of the stone marker to align with the viewing area, and overall, I think it's a really nice improvement that blends well with the site but vastly improves visitor safety. ADA accessibility to the site is also very much improved."

Powered in part by the very presence and exploits of Prefontaine, on the shoulders of decades of track excellence beforehand and also the champions and championships afterward, Eugene has earned a certain moniker of pride: Track Town USA.

It was only natural that Eugene would be so labeled due to its running heritage. Over time, the Oregon city was being referenced as "Track Town" as *the* destination for track and field. Eventually, in 2013, a nonprofit organization named Track Town USA, Inc., was officially incorporated.

According to its mission statement, "Track Town USA, Inc. is a non-profit organization committed to setting a standard of excellence in the sports of track and field and running by hosting premier events, creating a supportive environment for elite athletic performances, improving facilities, being a leader in sustainability, and inspiring the next generation of track and field athletes and fans."

*Chapter 4*

# HAYWARD FIELD, COLLEGE, POST-COLLEGIATE...

Situated at the northeast corner of East 15th Avenue and Agate Street in Eugene, Oregon, was the on-campus heart of track and field at the University of Oregon (UO). Originally built for the football team, Historic Hayward Field eventually became solely the home of the Fighting Duck track runners and field athletes.

Nineteen years after UO opened, its track and field began in 1895 and dual meets five years later. Just after the turn of the century, the team started to compete on a 440-yard dirt track at Kincaid Field (Memorial Quadrangle at 13th Avenue and Kincaid Street), named after sixth Oregon Secretary of State Harrison Rittenhouse Kincaid.

The sport was guided by five coaches over its first nine years: Joseph Wetherbee (1895), William O'Trine (1896), J.C. Higgins (1897), O'Trine (1898–1901), C.A. Redmond (1902), and William Ray (1903). In 1904, Michigan-born, Canadian-raised William "Colonel Bill" Hayward, an elite-level athlete in boxing, ice hockey, lacrosse, rowing, track, and wrestling, was hired away from Oregon's Albany College (Lewis and Clark College in Portland, Oregon) as UO's first long-term track and field coach.

About a dozen or so years into Hayward's stewardship, it was evident that his thinclads required a new track, as the sport was steadily growing and prospering. Shortly after a stoppage for the Great War, the first step was a new stadium for the football team, built on a cow pasture utilized to collect milk for students. At the first pigskin game, in 1919, the gridiron home was dedicated as Hayward Field, but the namesake was initially unaware of the honor because as the team's trainer he was in the locker room during the halftime ceremony.

In 1921, encircling the football field was built a cinder track of six lanes, which included at the east side a straightaway of 220 yards. In the 1920s and 1930s, bleachers and grandstands were built and refined; the field of sawdust was replaced by turf; and an addition was built at the south end.

Coach Hayward, after forty-four years—which included him coaching four WR (world record) holders, six AR holders, nine Olympians, and six U.S. Olympic Track teams (1908-32)—retired in the fall of 1947. He died a few months later, on December 14, at the age of seventy-nine.

Next to helm track was UO basketball and football coach John Warren, for one year. Then, in 1949, UO alumnus and decorated U.S. Army major Bill Bowerman, after several years as a football and track coach at Oregon schools in Portland and Medford, became the eighth coach.

Around this time, in the late 1940s, additional renovations to Hayward Field yielded permanent and removeable seats for football game full houses of 22,500 and the installation of a new electronic scoreboard in 1949. Shortly thereafter, in the 1950s, more work was done on the grandstands and bleachers.

After forty-seven years of calling Hayward Field home, the last football game was played there in November 1966. Nine months later, UO played its first game at the newly built Autzen Stadium. Named after Oregon State University (OSU) philanthropist and lumber manufacturer Thomas J. Autzen—whose son and foundation president Thomas E. Autzen attended UO—the forty-one-thousand-seat arena is about three miles north of Hayward Field, on the other side of Willamette River, at 2700 Martin Luther King Jr. Boulevard in Eugene.

Finally, according to UO Athletics, in 1970 was when Hayward Field was first "designated solely for track and field." This was also a time when Hayward Field welcomed two major trajectorial additions: on April 29, 1969, Steve Prefontaine signed his letter of intent to attend UO and join the Fighting Ducks; and in 1970, the cinder track was replaced and upgraded to an all-weather surface of Pro-Turf urethane over asphalt (the oval was named Stevenson Track in honor of Donald and Angeline Stevenson, whose contributions provided the necessary financial support).

It took forty-three years before Hayward Field held its first title event, the 1962 NCAA Men's Outdoor Track and Field Championships. But by the time it hosted the global World Athletics Championships sixty years later, in 2022—the first time in the United States for the former IAAF

October 30, 1967

Mr. Steve Prefontaine
Marshfield High School
Coos Bay, Oregon

Dear Steve:

Bill Dellinger and I have watched the newspaper with interest this fall in your cross-country races. We congratulate you on your steady improvement.

On the afternoon of October 27, I was laying out the cross-country course for the meet with Oregon State, while Bill Dellinger was out to watch the District Championship. Bill reports, as do Roscoe Divine and Dave Wilborn, a couple of Oregon sub-four-minute milers, that you look like a real champion.

Congratulations, hit the books and if we can be of help to you here at the University of Oregon, we would be more than pleased to do so.

Sincerely,

W. J. Bowerman
Professor of Physical Education
Track Coach

sk
cc: Walt McClure

University of Oregon coach Bill Bowerman's letter of October 30, 1967, to Steve Prefontaine. *University Archives photograph, University Photographic Collection, University of Oregon Libraries Special Collections and University Archives 3203.*

championships—Hayward Field had played host to a staggering site-record six U.S. Olympic Track and Field Team Trials (1972, 1976, 1980, 2008, 2012, 2016), the 2014 IAAF World Junior Athletics U20 Championships (first time in the United States), seven national USATF Championships (1986, 1993, 1999, 2001, 2009, 2011, 2015), a site-record seventeen NCAA Men's Outdoor Track and Field Championships (1962, 1964, 1972, 1978, 1984, 1988, 1991, 1996, 2001, 2010, 2013-18, 2021), and a site-record thirteen NCAA Women's Outdoor Track and Field Championships (1984, 1988, 1991, 1996, 2001, 2010, 2013-18, 2021).

Prefontaine reportedly first stepped foot on Hayward Field as a seventeen-year-old Marshfield High School (MHS) upperclassman in August 1968, eight months before he committed to UO. As future fellow teammate and roommate Pat Tyson recalls, "I was invited down from Tacoma, Washington, to watch a low-altitude elite track meet that was put on at Hayward. And Steve was invited. He was a year younger than me and was going to be a senior in high school, and I was a freshman-to-be in college. University of Oregon coach Bill Dellinger invited me, and Steve and I roomed together in a dorm on campus."

While he received his diploma in 1974, during his UO athletic career that spanned from 1969 to 1973, Prefontaine recorded an unprecedented collegiate slate. At his Hayward Field home, he was 35-3, for a 92 percent win rate. And he also went undefeated in cross-country after his freshman year.

While some rookies, rubes, or novices may desire to ride under the radar for a while until a taste of success awakens their confidence, on the heels of a record-setting high school career and international experience representing the United States, Prefontaine charged right out of the gate with purpose. As an example, within a span of just eight weeks during his freshman year (May 2 to June 20), there was no doubt as to what to expect from him, as he let it be known who he was.

On May 2, 1970, Prefontaine ran a 4:00.4-winning mile at Hayward Field versus OSU. A month later, he continued his rise with his first sub-4:00 mile at the Oregon Twilight Meet on June 5, at Hayward Field, where he finished 1.1 seconds behind UO 4x1 mile relay WR-holder Roscoe Divine (3:56.3) with a 3:57.4, as the seventh Duck and thirty-seventh American to record the feat.

Five days later, in front of the U.S. House of Representatives, U.S. Representative John Dellenback of Oregon entered the accomplishment into the public U.S. Congressional Report.

In the June 15, 1970 issue of *Sports Illustrated*, the nineteen-year-old appeared in a full-cover photo and story that declared "America's Distance Prodigy: Freshman Steve Prefontaine." Less than a week after it hit the newsstands, on June 20 at the 1970 NCAA Outdoor Track and Field Championships in Des Moines, Iowa, at Drake University, he won the first of his seven combined NCAA titles, with a 13:22.0. Adding to the amazement, he ran on a foot that needed stitches from when he reportedly cut it open on a jagged bolt at a diving board at the swimming pool in his team's motel days earlier.

At the 1971 AAU Track and Field Championships at Historic Hayward Field, Steve Prefontaine (254) leads Frank Shorter. *University Archives photograph, UA Ref3, University of Oregon Libraries Special Collections and University Archives UA_REF_3_A_ATHPRE0017rb.*

And once again in his young life, Prefontaine made it in the public U.S. Congressional Record when U.S. Senator Bob Bennett of Utah mentioned the meet and stated, "The other NCAA meet record went to a freshman, Steve Prefontaine of Oregon, who blazed out a 13:22.0 three-mile. The old record was 13:38.8 set by Gerry Lindgren of Washington State."

On whatever level—school, city, state, nation—Prefontaine made news. He was that vibrant and enigmatic. And he loved to play the crowd, tease the competition, and rule the roost, which also caught the attention of his fellow Ducks, including Steve Bence.

"Perhaps the most poignant memory is the energy that Pre brought to the track," Bence recalled. "I compared it to bullfights that I went to while a high school student in Spain. Pre entering the tracks was like the bull entering the ring. [When] he would burst onto the track it seemed that all heads would turn and the excitement and anticipation in the place would take off. He helped create a very special environment."

In the Olympic year of 1972, Prefontaine highlights at Hayward Field included his 3:56.7-winning mile at the Oregon Twilight Meet on April 23, which ranked him tenth in the nation; an AR 13:29.6 in the 5,000 meters versus Washington State University (WSU) on April 29; a PR 3:39.8 in the 1,500 meters versus OSU on May 6; and a pair of victorious 5,000-meter wins at the 1972 NCAA Outdoor Track and Field Championships on June 1 (14:01.4 heat) and June 3 (13:31.4 final).

Thanks to Bowerman's supervision and Dellinger's execution, with a peak for the 1972 U.S. Olympic Track and Field Team Trials at Hayward Field as the specific goal, Prefontaine was the top American from 1,500 meters to 10,000 meters. His targeted training was on schedule.

For eleven days in the summer of 1972, from June 29 to July 9, Hayward Field played host to its first U.S. Olympic Track and Field Team Trials. In front of his homefield crowd, Prefontaine fed off his "People," as much as they fed off his energy. They carried each other in thunderous support— Pre's People vocally, Prefontaine physically.

On July 6, he won his 5,000-meter heat in 13:51.2, ahead of 1968 U.S. Olympian Tracy Smith (2nd, 13:52.8), Lindgren (3rd, 13:53.6), and Villanova University All-American Dick Buerkle (4th, 13:55.4).

Three days later, on July 9, in front of an SRO packed house on the last of the eight days of elite competition, Prefontaine reached his goal and qualified for the 1972 Munich Olympic Summer Games 5,000 meters with a fourth-world-best AR-winning 13:22.8, ahead of fellow qualifiers three-time (1960-68) U.S. Olympian George Young (2nd, 13:29.4) and University of Houston world top-ten three-miler Leonard Hilton (3rd, 13:40.2). Lindgren took an early lead, but then Prefontaine hit two miles at 8:46.0, three miles at 12:54.4 and, with confidence, covered the final 172 meters in 28.4 seconds (5,000 meters equals 3.1 miles).

Around this time, *Track & Field News* even made note of what it termed "Pre-Mania," which for some time had been manifested in T-shirts, license plates, and signs that showed the slogan "Go Pre!" Constant chants also arose whenever Prefontaine appeared and "warmed up" the crowd. And in an added good-natured exclamation, a few fans reportedly created white T-shirts with STOP PRE in a red octagon traffic-sign design for the Olympic Trials. Lindgren actually sported one as he warmed up. Prefontaine himself, handed a shirt during his routine victory lap, joined in the non-self-effacing attention after his win. *Track & Field News* had also featured an Olympic preview in which it said he would medal—gold, silver, or bronze—in that order of prediction!

Prefontaine departed Hayward Field for Munich's Olympic Stadium and the Games of the XX Olympiad in Germany. On September 7, he qualified

Scoreboard
at Historic
Hayward
Field. *Photo by
Paul Clerici.*

for the 5,000-meter final with a second-place 13:32.6 in his heat (Hilton and Young did not advance out of their heats).

In the 5,000-meter final, on September 10, the twenty-one-year-old battled mightily against eventual gold medalist Lasse Viren of Finland (13:26.4), silver medalist Mohamed Gammoudi of Tunisia (13:27.4), and bronze medalist Ian Stewart of Great Britain (13:27.6), as he finished fourth in 13:28.4, just eight-tenths off the medal stand. Prefontaine then followed the Olympics with a couple meets in Italy and England before he returned home.

East Grandstand area of Historic Hayward Field. *Photo by Paul Clerici.*

Despondent about his Olympic showing, he did reach out to family and friends. As Pre was a prolific letter and postcard writer, one of those correspondences he sent was to his UO fraternity brother and friend John Kaegi.

"He let me know what great condition he was in before the 1972 Munich Olympics, where he fully expected to win a gold medal in the 5K," said Kaegi. "We all saw how that dream was deflated, first by [athletes initially] being quarantined to [their] dorm room during the terrorist incident—which thoroughly depressed him and which happened on the other side of the same [complex] where he was staying. And the rest of the field…conspired to trap him into the pack for most of the race. By the time Steve emerged from the pack, he did not have enough time to develop the commanding lead he needed and fell to a fourth-place finish."

As he always intended, he did not run in the 1972 collegiate cross-country season in order to regroup and recharge (and use the eligibility for 1973 cross-country). His first meets after the Olympic Games and Europe meets were in indoor track.

After his 1973 indoor track season, which included a two-mile win in Los Angeles over 1968 U.S. Olympian and 1971 Pan American 1,500-meter gold medalist Marty Liquori, Prefontaine, in what he described as a period of post-Olympic "rest," still included weeks of seventy to ninety miles—despite experiencing some injuries—and continued his running regime.

For indoors, Prefontaine's two-mile slate was impressive. He lost only one of the eight in which he ran and recorded four of the top six sub-8:30 American times!

His undefeated 1973 collegiate outdoor track season included a coaching change when, a day before the second meet, Bowerman, on March 23, officially retired, shortly after he had first reduced his daily role in 1972. He had a twenty-four-year Hall of Fame career.

Hayward Field was not aging well. In 1972, UO was notified of inspectors' serious concerns about its sustainability and its need of restoration. Bowerman realized his time could not fairly be split between coaching athletes and fundraising to help that restoration process. As a result, in part, he decided he needed to focus on the university's push to replace and restore parts of the structure.

In June 2000, six months after Bowerman passed away at the age of eighty-eight, a Diana Lee Jackson–created statue of him was dedicated at Hayward Field. Standing atop a platform of waffle grates, he is looking at his timer's watch while overlooking the track.

The "new" coach was named as Dellinger, three-time All-American Duck, five-year UO assistant coach, three-time U.S. Olympian, and 1964 Tokyo Olympic Summer Games 5,000-meter bronze medalist.

Among Prefontaine's wins were an AR 27:09.4 in the six-mile at the Bakersfield All-Comers Meet on May 24; an unprecedented same-day WR double (3:56.8 mile and, on an hour's rest, a 13:06.4 three-mile) at a home quad-meet between UCLA, University of Nebraska, UO, and WSU on April 14; a national third-best and world ninth-best 3:55.0 mile at the Oregon Twilight Meet in Eugene on April 27; the Pac-8 Conference Championship three-mile title (13:10.4) in Eugene on May 19; the 1973 NCAA Outdoor Track and Field Championship three-mile heat (MR 13:19.0) and final (13:05.3), as the first to win four consecutive outdoor titles, in Baton Rouge, Louisiana; and the 1973 AAU Outdoor Track and Field Championship three-mile heat (13:17.8) and final (world sixth-best 12:53.4) in Bakersfield, California.

Prefontaine then returned to UO for the first fundraising Hayward Field Restoration Meet, on June 20, 1973. In front of an estimated twelve thousand fans, and just four days after his AAU AR, he helped pace U.S. Olympic gold medalist Dave Wottle to a PR-winning 3:53.3 mile in only

West Grandstand area of Historic Hayward Field. *Photo by Carol Hunt-Clerici.*

his third defeat in that distance, as he finished second in a PR 3:54.6. While Prefontaine had originally invited the gold-medal Olympian to try and help Wottle set a WR, the fast pace nevertheless yielded seven of the runners to sub-4:00 times.

In 1974, after a few mile and two-mile wins to open his outdoor track season, Prefontaine took on the 1974 Oregon Twilight Meet in Eugene on April 27 with a six-mile AR 26:51.8 en route to a world sixth-best and AR 27:43.6 in the 10,000 meters (6.2 miles), a distance he requested instead of the six-mile. This was in front of "only" seven thousand fans due to the West Grandstand having been bulldozed during its restoration.

At the second Hayward Field Restoration Meet, on June 8, 1974, Prefontaine won the three-mile with a late-surge world third-best and AR 12:51.4 over 1972 U.S. Olympic Marathon gold medalist Frank Shorter's runner-up 12:52.0.

"It was planned for he and I to try to break the American record for three miles, which at the time was 12:53 by Gerry Lindgren," noted Shorter. "I got out there and we planned to share half-miles, and I think I took the first one. And Bill Bowerman was at the 200-meter mark, and we're getting 200 splits for pace. The difficulty with that race was we were running 64 (for laps) and the wind was blowing so hard down the homestretch in our faces that we ran [half laps at] 31, 33, 31, 33. With a half-mile to go—our agreement was, every man for himself—he was leading two laps from the end. And I didn't go by him. And people thought, I guess for a while, they said, 'Well, he should have gone by him.' I said, 'No, no, no. If you watched how we ran the race, every time we shift-and-lead, the person in front would go out and you'd go in on the inside.' With two laps to go, he didn't pull out because he knew I wasn't coming through. He knew the race was on. Going into the final turn, I actually had a 10-yard lead on him down the backstretch. In Eugene! And all I could think of was we're going to round that turn and come into that homestretch and he's going to be coming! I knew he was there and when he came by. He passed me a yard from the finish line, maybe two yards. And here's where it's obvious [about our friendship], he finished the race and the minute he hit the finish line he started to turn around, took a step or two and stopped, and hugged me as I came across the finish line. He broke the American record and I ran faster than the old American record, so that was when we became friends."

On September 3, 1974, Prefontaine gathered together some teammates from his Oregon Track Club (OTC) for an unofficial mile at Hayward Field, where a reported nearly one thousand fans showed up to watch their famous native son. As a tune-up for his European meets, which he often did with a mile race, he pushed hard for a 3:58.3 win. It wasn't necessarily the competition he battled that day, though, but the air quality.

The timing of the race coincided with the decades-old accepted practice in Oregon of when seed farmers burn their fields between roughly mid-July to mid-September. According to a December 1974 OSU Research in Field Burning report, field burning reduces potential seed and grass diseases, eliminates field residue, increases seed yields, and controls weeds, among other benefits. However, the quality of the air over nearby communities cannot be managed 100 percent of the time when between four thousand and ten thousand acres are burned and wind direction can unexpectedly change in Willamette Valley.

On that day, known as "Black Tuesday," wind direction did indeed shift, warnings were issued, and the track was noticeably partially hidden and appeared lost in heavy, dense smoke. It caused Prefontaine afterward to cough so vigorously that he coughed up blood and subsequently tore muscles under his ribcage (which was not fully diagnosed until later). This heavily affected his European meets on September 10 in Finland and September 13 in England, the last of which he was forced to drop out due to the muscle damage (a first in his illustrious career). He later joined others and spoke in front of the Oregon State Senate to ban field burning.

After his 1975 indoors, Prefontaine in outdoors at the Oregon Twilight Meet in Eugene on April 26 ran the nation's sixth-fastest six-mile time

Historic Hayward Field. *Photo by Carol Hunt-Clerici.*

(27:18.6) on his way to the fifth-fastest U.S. time in the 10,000 meters (28:09.4).

Around this time, a project that occupied much of his energy was a series of meets between American athletes and Finnish athletes. As Pre was the organizer of the invited visit, his main focus was to bring Europe to the United States in much the same way as when he and fellow Americans often traveled to compete in European and Scandinavian meets.

The result was a series of 1975 spring meets at Madras High School in Madras, Oregon (May 4); MHS in Coos Bay, Oregon (May 9); Burnaby in Canada (May 15); California Relays in Modesto, California (May 24); and NCAA Preparation Meet at Hayward Field (May 29).

At Madras, he won the 3,000 meters in 8:26.4. He followed that with his last AR, fittingly on his high school track at MHS, with a 5:01.4 in the 2,000 meters. The third stop was the previously scheduled British Columbia International Meet in Canada, where he won the 5,000 meters in 13:46.8. Nine days later was also the previously scheduled 1975 California Relays in Modesto, where he won the two-mile in 8:36.4.

Just prior to the final meet—the NCAA Prep—Prefontaine turned to a friend to help in the absence of invited Finnish rival Viren, who canceled due to injury.

"He called me up the Wednesday before the meet against the Finns and said, 'Can you come out and race me in two days, on Friday?' Two days!" recalled Shorter of Prefontaine's call. "I'd just gotten back from doing intervals, and I was in my kitchen, and I said, 'Oh, you need somebody to beat, huh!' Viren had dropped out. So I went out and we ran the race."

On May 29, in front of an estimated seven to eight thousand fans at Hayward Field in the NCAA Prep, Prefontaine ran the 5,000 meters. Behind rabbit Ducks Paul Geis and Terry Williams, Shorter led at the first mile (4:18) and the second mile (8:40.5). Prefontaine, who did lead a few laps, finally turned it on and won with a 60.3 bell lap in 13:23.8, with Shorter second at 13:32.2.

Shorter always knew he would need a large lead when he competed against his friend.

"I never hung in and kicked because I knew I was never the fastest guy in the race, no matter what the distance. I had to get ahead of him. I just didn't want to be within about three, four seconds. My best 400, my best last lap in a 5,000 was in the national three-mile when I won it in 1970. I ran 54.9 for my last 400, which isn't bad for a marathoner. And Steve could have run 52, 53, so I had to be at least three seconds ahead if I was going to [contend]. That's what I'd try to do," noted Shorter, who always appreciated his training with Prefontaine despite their different tactics. "My focus was what we had in common and how we could help each other, and we both knew that. You get better training with someone of equal or better ability than you do by yourself—you both get better—and we both knew that. Even though there was the [four-year] age difference, that didn't mean anything to me because what was important was the level of performance. And we were in slightly different disciplines; he had not decided to run the 10,000 yet [when they first began to train together], and his fiber was a little bit different from mine because my best mile is 4:02.6 and his best mile's 3:54.6. So I think it wasn't that we really had that much of a rivalry, but I think maybe it was because I'd run 5,000 meters against him and let's just see what happens. If I lost, at least I'd be running fast. And I think we both enjoyed that. We had a sense of what sharing meant. It's equal, it's even."

Tragically, approximately four hours after his win, shortly after 12:30 a.m. on May 30, Prefontaine died in a car accident on Skyline Boulevard, about a mile and a half east of UO.

The following few days—in Eugene, in Coos Bay, in Oregon, in the United States, throughout the world—leading up to the memorial services were a blur of shock, sadness, and mourning.

Historic Hayward Field East Grandstand. *Photo by Carol Hunt-Clerici.*

The day after the funeral service and burial in his hometown of Coos Bay, an estimated four thousand people gathered at Hayward Field on June 3 to mourn and to celebrate his rich life. Those who spoke included Bowerman, Moore, and Shorter. In his eulogy, which has been included in the public U.S. Congressional Record archives, Moore focused on many aspects of Prefontaine, among them his artistry, commitment, and determination.

"He conceived of his sport as a service in the way an artist serves. Without that, he would never have given us all the records. They were out beyond winning or losing, which a runner does for himself. They came from those furious minutes near the end of a race when his relentlessness and his People's excitement got all scrambled together in that thrilling madness. All of us who have said in these past few days, 'I had no idea how much this man meant to me,' have done so because we had not realized how much we meant to him. He was our glory, and we his," Moore stated, in part. "Commensurate with the ferocity of his loyalty to us, to Oregon, to working people, to those he respected, was the severity of his resistance to those who had not won his respect. He most visibly embodied that streak of defiance that must be in all runners. He bucked the traditions of accumulation and power, for the freedom of his own way."

And as planned beforehand, the scoreboard clock was set at 12:36.2, a worthy three-mile goal of Prefontaine's. For the final minute, and for the final time, people cheered on their favorite son.

Eight days after he passed away, Prefontaine was honored again at Hayward Field. To recognize UO's retired coach, the upcoming third annual Hayward Field Restoration Meet was renamed the Bill Bowerman Classic and scheduled for June 7, 1975. However, in light of the recent tragedy, it was agreed upon by all those involved, including Bowerman, to instead name it the Steve Prefontaine Classic.

Since the 1975 edition, the Prefontaine Classic annually features Hall of Fame track and field athletes as well as collegiate, state, national, and world records. Thanks especially to the guidance of former *Track & Field News* scribe Tom Jordan, who shortly after he moved to Eugene became the race director in 1984 for nearly forty years, he and his team put on one of the greatest annual shows on earth. Part of the former IAAF Grand Prix circuit of worldwide meets, it was also included among the international Diamond League calendar, including its series final in 2023.

In the years and decades since Prefontaine's passing, Hayward Field has taken on an even more mystical, magical quality. There appears a tangible

Historic Hayward Field West Grandstand. *Photo by Paul Clerici.*

spirit in the air. It is always on the list of places to visit. But after nearly one hundred years, and several patchworks and repairs over the decades, it was finally determined to replace Historic Hayward Field. During the summer months of 2018, construction began.

According to UO, "Seeds for the Hayward project began with the need to renovate a storied-but-aging facility that was the venue for an ever-growing list of the sport's most-prominent events…but which lacked the infrastructure and amenities increasingly needed to host such events. The design team initially sought to preserve Hayward Field's landmark east grandstand. Because of numerous factors—a failing structure, noncompliance with the Americans with Disabilities Act, tight seating, obstructed sightlines, and virtually no amenities—…a unanimous conclusion [came] to look to the future and take a bold, innovative approach. Elements of the grandstand have been incorporated into the new facility to preserve the rich heritage of the original stadium through stories in exhibits and graphics."

Some of the highlights include a new main entrance of Powell Plaza; an improved nine-lane track; modern facilities and practice areas for athletes; wider seats and unobstructed views for spectators; historical exhibits; and a ten-story tower that depicts on its exterior several huge images, including one of Prefontaine.

As with any major project that involves the razing of an original—especially a historic site that spanned generations and became engrained in the fabric of the community, as well as being beloved in the hearts of those who called it home in one way or another—the decision to demolish Historic Hayward Field to create another Hayward Field was met with myriad emotions.

Some denied its need of improvement; some were angry at those who pushed forward with its replacement; some perhaps bargained to save part of it instead of destroying it all; some felt depressed that that corner of the world would no longer look and feel the same; and eventually, at some point in time, it is hoped all will accept its presence.

For athletes who competed on Stevenson Track inside Historic Hayward Field, especially those who spent their academic years at UO and rarely missed a date with the oval, opinions vary for a variety of reasons.

The first time that UO All-American Jordan Hasay was at Hayward Field, she was a high school phenom out of California who had already set multiple NRs and received Athlete of the Year honors. Her 1,500-meter runs at the 2008 U.S. Olympic Women's Track and Field Team Trials at

University of Oregon's Hayward Field. *Courtesy University of Oregon.*

Historic Hayward Field garnered national attention and endearment from the crowd, who chanted her name to become a Duck. She ran a 4:18.39 in the preliminary, a high school NR 4:14.50 in her semifinal, and a tenth-place 4:17.36 in the final.

"When I was sixteen years old, we drove to the track and [with no one there] we went up into the grandstands. And I started crying because I told my mom, 'I can't run in front of all these people. I'm so scared,'" Hasay recalled of her first trip to UO. "And then I went out and set a high school national record [over] the next days. So that's a good reminder that I always kind of feel like that before races. And, of course, I had some very magical moments there."

By the time she signed her letter of intent to UO in 2009, Hasay knew the track's history and appreciated it even more as a Duck.

"It was just an honor to be an athlete there because you knew that the crowd was always going to be behind you, for all the athletes," she said. "It's nice when the crowd understands what you do and the preparation behind it and they understand the tactics of certain races; especially for the long-distance runners, they appreciate something like the 10K, which is twenty-five laps around. That was really, really special. Great memories. I would compare it to marathoning for Boston is like what track and field is like for Hayward; the fans are so knowledgeable."

Former Duck Parker Stinson has plenty of experience on Historic Hayward Field, as a twelve-year-old at the 2004 USATF National Junior Olympic Track and Field Championships to a high school runner in the U.S. Junior Championships to three NCAA team titles at UO.

"My first impression was it was like a gladiator arena—it got my heart going," he said with excitement. "And just knowing the legendary people that had run there before was just kind of crazy; and to be literally running in their footsteps! It just seemed like no other track stadium I'd ever been in. There was just something about the crowds in the Hayward stadium—how packed they get, how loud they get—and the stomping of the wood [stands]. What was so cool was how the stadium and the crowd were just one. It was just so loud. Even as a fan sitting in the crowd and cheering people on was really exciting. It was interactive. Kind of felt like a concert. Going there was a dream; being an Oregon Duck for five years was incredible."

Nell Rojas, who ran for Northern Arizona University, recalls how she felt when she competed at Historic Hayward Field as a freshman at the 2007 NCAA Women's West Region Outdoor Track and Field Championships.

"I definitely recognized the history of Hayward Field, especially because my dad ran for Nike back in the day and knew Pre," she said, in reference to her father, 15K world record-setter (1981) and U.S. AAU Cross-Country Championships winner (1976) Ric Rojas. "So I grew up knowing that history and learning it and being really interested in it. The first time I ran at Hayward was in college, in the old field. It was a great experience. Really fun. I was humbled to be there, I was happy to be there, but you take it in and then you're focused on the race. But there are times with the athletes that are walking around you; when you walk past people that you've looked up to forever and you're like, 'Well, I'm right here! That's kind of crazy, but okay!'"

Ric Rojas, who coaches his daughter, vividly recalls Prefontaine, who even mailed him a handwritten recruiting letter.

"He was an old soul. He had really broad world views on issues having greater impact than on just the running, but the running was where he started," he says. "He'd talk about amateurism, coaching—he had very strong opinions about coaching. He was beyond his years, even as a teenager. Extremely talented, related well to kids, and was just a regular guy. He understood the value of being an influence. He was a very complex person."

Hayward Field. *Photo by Mike Fanelli.*

U.S. Olympian Molly Huddle, who has competed in the USATF Outdoor Track and Field Championships at Historic Hayward Field and finished in the top ten in the 10,000 meters (ninth) and 5,000 meters (tenth) at the 2008 U.S. Olympic Women's Track and Field Team Trials there as well, has overall fond memories.

"I do remember being very overwhelmed by all the history and the way the fans show up there; it was a little bit overwhelming. I'd been to [the 2004 U.S. Olympic Women's Track and Field Team Trials in] Sacramento, but Eugene was very different," she remembered. "You walk in and you just feel the respect for track and field and you just feel how big the event is. I actually had a bad experience my first time, so I had to learn to love Hayward because I thought maybe it was bad luck. I had since been to Hayward Field many times and have had some of my most memorable races there."

Huddle does miss Historic Hayward Field, especially the configuration of how the grandstands seem to physically reach over to the athletes.

"You felt it, that everyone was excited to see you. That was a nice part about the grandstand being what they were; they held a lot of people, but they weren't like the spaceship-type stadiums we have now. Like at the World Championships or Olympics, a lot of it was empty. The bigger stadiums are just like a blur; they're fancy, and I know you have to keep up with the times, but I appreciate the old Hayward," said Huddle, who liked the closeness of the fans. "I could hear my parents at Hayward, I could hear my coach. And it always feels like a dream when you're there because they always have those big clouds floating around so you feel like you're in a snow globe, like an old memory is happening now. They have their own atmosphere. That's how I think of Eugene!"

During the extended construction and worldwide COVID-19 pandemic hiatus, Hayward Field went unused. The 2019 Prefontaine Classic was held at Cobb Track and Angell Field on June 30 at Stanford University. And due to the pandemic, the 2020 Prefontaine Classic was not held.

The "reimagined" Hayward Field finally (re)opened for competition in April 2021. That year also included the 2020 U.S. Olympic Track and Field Team Trials in June (Olympic events always include the Olympiad year, regardless of when it is held) and the Prefontaine Classic on August 21, 2021, sans spectators and under strict regulations and guidelines.

As someone who has run on both Hayward Field tracks, Nell Rojas, who competed in the 2020 U.S. Olympic Women's Trials 10,000 meters, has mixed feelings about each.

Steve Prefontaine artwork inside Hayward Field. *Photo by Mike Fanelli.*

"It's a great new facility," she said. "It's really impressive in a different way. You're honored to be there, especially with something like the Olympic Trials. It's kind of like the same as when you went to the old Hayward and it was like, 'Wow, I'm a part of history.' With the new one, it's different. To me, it's not the historical Hayward. I was very disappointed that they were tearing it down. I still can't believe…I mean, if I were to go to the University of Oregon, I would be like 'Yes, this is awesome! I want this track!' But as an outsider who's not there, I wish they kept the old one."

Regarding the difference between the two facilities, Hasay recalled talking about it with teammates.

"We always joke that the Oregon team is spoiled now because they have all this stuff—a nail salon down there, they've got TVs, couches," Hasay said with a laugh. "When we were there, it was just these crappy old stretch mats and a speaker that someone brought in that they got on eBay. But I kind of liked that. It was more like bring it yourself. I don't know if I would like how fancy it is now. And they had Tinker Hatfield, the shoe designer from Nike, did a talk for them! Now they get all this special treatment and stuff, and we never had that. And we would just run around the turf fields up there and the little 200-meter practice track sometimes, but we would do our warmup on the route there. It's funny how things have evolved and changed. I feel old now. I graduated in 2013; it's crazy!"

Somalian-born American Abdi Abdirahman, a Prefontaine Classic veteran who won the 2008 U.S. Olympic Track and Field Team Trials 10,000 meters at Historic Hayward Field, has kind words for both tracks.

"Whenever anyone talk about Hayward Field, first thing that come to mind is Prefontaine Classic because for me, it's the same track that Pre ran. It's just the history behind that—Bill Bowerman, Pre, Bob Kennedy, Todd Williams; these people that come before us. I am where I am because of them. I get it," said the five-time U.S. Olympian. "[Historic] Hayward Field is like a Yankee Stadium, historic Madison Square Garden—a landmark for track and field. It was cozy. But you need to upgrade. I went to the Trials and I saw the new stadium, and I knew it was amazing, wonderful. People always want to preserve the history, but sometimes you got to upgrade. And I think they used some of the old building for the new building. Everything is brand new, but at the end of the day, you have to upgrade. For me to see a facility like that, as a track runner and a track fan, it was amazing. I like everything about it. It's a top facility."

Paige Stoner, who for Syracuse University won bronze in the 3,000-meter steeplechase at the 2018 NCAA Women's Outdoor Track and Field

Championships at Historic Hayward Field, also ran in the 2020 U.S. Olympic Women's Track and Field Team Trials 10,000 meters at UO in June 2021.

"The old stadium was incredible, and it's incredible what they've turned it into. I knew it was going to be a huge upgrade, but you really need to be there and take it in for yourself to understand how big it has become. They really did a great job of showcasing the history of our sport and what's gone down in Hayward Field in the last one hundred years," she observed. "I was in the [Olympic Trials] 10K, and it was one of the races that got changed to the morning time, so I got to spectate one of the days. It's really spread out and it's just very open. It's really cool to see they would make something like that for track and field here. You hear about stadiums like that over in Europe, but to have it here on our home soil is really neat. The old one's special, for sure, and this one is special in a different way. We have this now, and we can hold these world championships, and there's no better place to have done it than Eugene."

# Chapter 5

# BEAVERTON, NIKE, OREGON SPORTS HALL OF FAME AND MUSEUM...

In 1964, Blue Ribbon Sports (BRS) was started by former University of Oregon (UO) runner Phil Knight and UO head coach Bill Bowerman. Primarily out of Eugene, Oregon, it distributed Onitsuka Company's Tiger running shoes from Japan. Just over seven years later, in 1971, Nike was officially born, and after also selling its own Nike Cortez shoes, in 1972 it eventually separated itself from Onitsuka.

Bowerman experimented with a new sole, which he wanted to be similar to the track surface itself (urethane) to increase cushion, absorption, and comfort and also reduce hard-sole-to-hard-track injuries. His first attempts included pouring the rubber substance into his wife's waffle irons due to its waffle-style grid. Further tests eventually led to reversing that grid to create inverted "nubs" and more control over managing the rubber slabs, which he successfully invented and later patented.

A big boost was having the 1972 U.S. Olympic Track and Field (and Marathon) Team Trials in Eugene.

Greater Boston Track Club (GBTC) coach Tom Derderian, who worked for Nike in the 1970s and '80s in product development and design, remembers the excitement surrounding the new running shoes; the Trials in Eugene (in which he ran the Marathon); and the nation's best all-around track town.

"We got these special, newly made first Nike waffle shoes. And what was impressive was being in a town where track is a major sport, which is a treat," said Derderian, who points to an earlier instance at Hayward Field when that rang true. "The first time I went to Eugene, I ran in an All-Comer meet

*Left*: University of Oregon coach Bill Bowerman statue. *Photo by Paul Clerici.*

*Below*: University of Oregon coach Bill Bowerman statue feature of waffle irons. *Photo by Paul Clerici.*

Waffle irons damaged by Bill Bowerman while working on early Nike running shoes. *Photo by T.K. Gore.*

on the track because some guys needed a qualifying time for the 400-meter intermediate hurdles and you have to have a certain number of people in the race [for it to count], so they asked me to be in the race. And I said sure. I'd run the steeplechase in college, so it was no trouble."

The star at the 1972 U.S. Olympic Trials, of course, was its home-state hero Steve Prefontaine, to whom Derderian was introduced by 1964 U.S. Olympian Gerry Lindgren.

Derderian recalled of Prefontaine, "We jogged around the practice track and talked about I don't know what, probably whatever we saw on the track that day. He was just one of the guys, and he was there to train and run. He was a regular-guy runner. Normal."

The first athlete paid to wear Nikes was Grand Slam-winning Romanian tennis player Ilie Nastase, followed by Prefontaine—the first runner.

Prefontaine, who wore early templates from Bowerman, earned a reported $5,000-a-year "stipend" from Nike to wear, promote, and present at clinics the new shoes. He called himself Nike's National Public Relations Manager and then National Director of Public Affairs on his business card, when BRS was still located at 6175 SW 112th Avenue, in Beaverton, Oregon.

Part of his responsibilities was to seek out and contact top runners and also mail Nikes. One such delivery made its way to Bill Rodgers, news of whose meteoric rise in Boston, Massachusetts, even appeared in the Oregon Track Club newsletter.

Around 1973-75, Rodgers was beginning to make a name for himself as a member of the dominant GBTC. Coached by future National Distance Running Hall of Fame Bill Bowerman Coaching Award recipient and USATF National Track and Field Hall of Fame coach Bill Squires, the twenty-five-year-old dropped out of his first attempt at the Boston Marathon, in 1973, but returned to the Patriots' Day race in 1974 and finished fourteenth.

As part of his training for the 1975 Boston Marathon, Squires had Rodgers train for and run in the IAAF World Cross-Country 12K (7.45 miles) Championship in Rabat, Morocco, five weeks before Boston. While the only American with a podium finish was in 1966 (Tracy Smith's bronze-medal 36:32.2), Squires recognized the value of this race.

Rodgers won bronze in an AR 35:27.4.

"I was on the plane with Frank Shorter and Jeff Galloway, and I was very psyched I won a bronze medal!" Rodgers recalls of his trip home with teammates. "I was telling Jeff and Frank that I was running Boston in a few

Wall of Nikes history display at Nike Worldwide Headquarters in Beaverton, Oregon. *Photo by Steve Bence.*

weeks, and I knew they were with Nike, and I asked, 'Can you get me some racing shoes?' I think it was Jeff who spoke with Pre, because he knew him from the Olympic team in 1972."

For the IAAF, Rodgers wore a pair of Asics he borrowed from teammate Gary Tuttle, who came to Rodgers's rescue.

"I'd forgotten my shoes on the trip," Rodgers notes with a laugh at an oft-occurrence.

About three weeks after Rabat, on April 9, 1975, twelve days before the Boston Marathon, Prefontaine drafted a letter to Rodgers and mailed it to him with Nike Obori Boston 73 running shoes, so named after Jon Anderson of Oregon, who won the 1973 Boston Marathon in a pair of Nike Oboris (named after Obori Park, Fukuoka, Japan).

Prefontaine wrote, "Dear Bill. First of all congratulations on a fine race in Rabat. You have really improved this last year and hopefully will continue to until the Olympic games. The reason I'm writing is because Jeff Galloway told me you were interested in training in our shoes. I'm sending you a pair of Boston 73's and a training shoe. Any comments would be greatly appreciated. Just feel free to drop me a line and let me know what you think. Wishing you continued success for 75. Sincerely, Steve Prefontaine."

Rodgers was thrilled.

"I was pretty wired. I was pretty psyched. I had just taken a medal. I beat Frank Shorter and a lot of the best runners in the world. So I knew I had a shot to do pretty well [at Boston]," noted Rodgers. "It was a perfect day, it was cool, it was my third Boston, so I knew the course by now. And everything went well."

And as far as that cardinal sin of running a race in new shoes, especially a marathon, Rodgers notes with a laugh, "Well, you know, I was running pretty high mileage (487 miles in April 1975) and I was twenty-seven years old and I was pretty strong at that time. You have your good days; seize the day!"

In those Nikes, Rodgers won the 1975 Boston Marathon in an AR/CR 2:09:55.

"They worked out great—won the race, no blisters!" proudly stated Rodgers, who also wore them at the 31.6K (19.6 miles) San Juan 450 in Puerto Rico in June, which he won in 1:45:03.

But Rodgers never met Prefontaine, whose fatal car accident in Eugene, Oregon, occurred twenty-nine days after the 1975 Boston Marathon.

"I wish I'd met him," Rodgers said wistfully. "I met some of his family when I was out there in Oregon. I just wish I had met Pre. Maybe we would

Bill Rodgers Running Center store display of the items from his 1975 Boston Marathon win, which includes the Nike running shoes he wore that were mailed to him by Steve Prefontaine. *Photo by Paul Clerici.*

have duked it out in world cross-country! But I kind of feel that I had met him in a certain way."

For decades, on display at the Bill Rodgers Running Center store at Faneuil Hall Marketplace in Boston were the letter, Nikes, New Balance headband, water bottle, and handwritten GBTC BOSTON shirt he wore in the race.

"The man who built the display case was Paul Sullivan. He did a lot of the carpentry when the store was put together," recalled Bill's brother Charlie Rodgers. "I still have it, along with the New Balance headband Bill wore; Nike did not seem to want it in the Nike display."

After the brick-and-mortar store closed in 2012, it was decided to "return" them to Nike Worldwide Headquarters (NWHQ) in Beaverton, Oregon.

"Finally, we went to Nike headquarters, which I'd never been to before, and returned the shoes to Nike," Rodgers said. "Carl Lewis was there. [Fellow GBTC teammate] Alberto [Salazar] was there, and some of my old friends from Jamaica Plain [Massachusetts]. Vinnie Fleming."

It was quite a reunion. And Rodgers also enjoyed the topics of conversation, which of course turned to Prefontaine.

Nike Worldwide Headquarters in Beaverton, Oregon. *Photo by Paul Clerici.*

"It was kind of a cool thing talking about what the sport was like and how we struggled without being paid for our efforts. Pre tried to change the sport. He and Shorter both…tried to fight and break the sport open so the sport could achieve the level of visibility in the United States and around the world that it deserved. There was a lot of backwardness and some corruption and pushing the athletes down, so Pre was a terrific leader," Rodgers noted.

After its beginnings in the 1980s on about seventy acres at Murray Boulevard in Beaverton, Oregon, NWHQ opened in 1990 at 1 Bowerman Way, about four miles northwest of where Prefontaine had worked.

One of the original eight buildings is named Steve Prefontaine Hall. Located on the south side of its campus, it is the centerpiece of the complex, which has grown to nearly three hundred acres of fields, tracks, trails, pools, courts, gyms, and dozens of buildings.

Steve Prefontaine Hall features several display cases of original Nike artifacts, memorabilia, waffle irons, and more; and Steve Prefontaine replica singlets, photos, and some original running shoes. And situated in the heart of its lobby, framed by bay windows and a backdrop of six-acre Lake Nike, is a larger-than-life statue of the Coos Bay icon.

Steve Prefontaine Hall at Nike Worldwide Headquarters in Beaverton, Oregon. *Photo by Paul Clerici.*

Lake Nike and Steve Prefontaine Hall at Nike Worldwide Headquarters in Beaverton, Oregon. *Photo by Paul Clerici.*

Located on the sides of the many buildings on the north and south sections of the campus are nearly three hundred plaques of coaches and athletes of note. Created by Denali Granholm, they compose the Walkway of Fame.

Among those featured is Squires, who in addition to having coached the likes of Derderian, Patti (Catalano) Dillon, and Rodgers, also coached Bruce Bickford, Dan Dillon, and Salazar before they departed GBTC for Athletics West in 1980; and Bob Sevene, who coached inaugural 1984 U.S. Olympic Women's Marathon gold medalist and two-time Boston winner Joan Benoit Samuelson.

"That was a surprise. A very nice honor," said Squires, who was also asked who he'd like at the ceremony. "I said I want my pals that all talked about what I'd done for running to be there. And they got a hold of anyone that could get out there. I never thought it would look so nice."

At the ceremony, Squires also enjoyed talking about Historic Hayward Field, which he had visited.

"The wood stands are right next to the track and they get on you from all sides," he marveled. "They're very educated about the sport, and they're

Steve Prefontaine display case at Nike Worldwide Headquarters in Beaverton, Oregon. *Photo by T.K. Gore.*

Steve Prefontaine display case at Nike Worldwide Headquarters in Beaverton, Oregon. *Photo by Paul Clerici.*

into track and field. They appreciate it. Very, very exciting—more exciting than you can believe. The people in the stands go crazy; they really eat it up. They want to be a part of that."

Also in the Beaver State is the Oregon Sports Hall of Fame and Museum (OSHFM). Founded in 1978, OSHFM has been housed in several locations over the years, including the twenty-seven-story Standard Insurance Center in Portland; a five-story office building on Salmon Street in Portland; and in Beaverton, about a mile and half north of where Prefontaine once worked for Nike.

Its website acts as a visual conduit to Oregon's rich sports history.

"The organization started out small; without staff or budget, it was literally just a group of extremely dedicated people. In 1980, that group selected the first class of inductees and an event developed from that—the Oregon Sports Hall of Fame Annual Induction Ceremony. Membership drives, board recruitment, and annual induction ceremonies followed, still with no paid staff or funding base. OSHFM gained strength and stature in these early years as a volunteer organization," according to its website. "In the beginning, the Hall of Fame's purpose was simply to preserve a rich legacy of athletic excellence in the state of Oregon. As the organization grew and evolved, the purpose evolved as well. The purpose today is best described by the Hall of Fame's mission statement—To recognize and appreciate Oregon's rich athletic history. Our goal is for this legacy to inspire

*Above*: Oregon Sports Hall of Fame and Museum exterior display when located in Portland, Oregon. *Photo by Paul Clerici.*

*Left*: Steve Prefontaine display at Oregon Sports Hall of Fame and Museum when housed in Portland, Oregon. *Photo by Paul Clerici.*

*Left*: Steve Prefontaine display at Oregon Sports Hall of Fame and Museum in its former Portland, Oregon site. *Photo by Paul Clerici.*

*Below*: Oregon Sports Hall of Fame and Museum display of Steve Prefontaine when located in Portland, Oregon. *Photo by Paul Clerici.*

participation in sport and foster awareness of the values and lifelong rewards gained from this participation."

Among the many sport-themed exhibits (baseball, basketball, track and field, football), theater experiences, and interactive programs, there's also the Roll of Honor that showcases Hall of Fame inductees, new classes of which are annually honored in induction ceremonies.

Some of those track and field athletes inducted since 1980 include Bowerman, Rudy Chapa, Bill Dellinger, Dick Fosbury, Bill Hayward, Kenny Moore, Prefontaine, Salazar, Mary Slaney, and Mac Wilkins.

*Chapter 6*

# PREFONTAINE AND

# WITHOUT LIMITS MOVIES

Since the early 1900s, movies have been filmed in Oregon, such as *The General* (Buster Keaton, 1926), *Paint Your Wagon* (Clint Eastwood, 1969), University of Oregon (UO) alumnus Ken Kesey's *One Flew Over the Cuckoo's Nest* (Jack Nicholson, 1975), *Batman Forever* (Val Kilmer, 1995), and *Wild* (Reese Witherspoon, 2014).

Among those filmed at UO include it as the fictional Faber College in *National Lampoon's Animal House* (John Belushi, 1978); Hayward Field, as itself during the actual 1980 U.S. Olympic Track and Field Team Trials, in *Personal Best* (Mariel Hemingway and UO's two-time U.S. Olympian Kenny Moore, 1982); and the made-for-TV-movie *Finish Line* (James Brolin, 1989).

Twenty years after Steve Prefontaine's death, CBS-TV led into its nationwide airing of the 1995 Prefontaine Classic with the Kesey-narrated documentary *Fire on the Track: The Steve Prefontaine Story*, by first-time director Erich Lyttle. It was co-written by Kesey, Lyttle, and Moore, and produced by Scott Chambers, Mark Doonan, former UO Duck Geoff Hollister, Jon Lutz, and Chris Petersen.

On the heels of renewed interest, the idea for a feature film about Prefontaine—which had been discussed for decades—began to develop again. When the negotiation dust settled, there were two of them!

They were both filmed during 1996. Hollywood Pictures of the Walt Disney Studios made *Prefontaine*, with Doonan, Hollister, and Lutz from the TV documentary; and the Cruise/Wagner Production team of Tom Cruise and Paula Wagner, powered by Warner Bros. Pictures, made *Without Limits*,

University of Oregon Erb Memorial Union student center and dining facility, where the food fight scene was filmed for *National Lampoon's Animal House. Photo by Paul Clerici.*

with Academy Award–winning director Robert Towne (*Chinatown*) and Moore, who had both worked together on *Personal Best*.

First released was the $8 million budget *Prefontaine*, in 1997. Directed by Steve James (*Hoop Dreams*) and co-written by the director and Eugene Corr, the movie unfolds over 107 minutes in a documentary-style approach of characters being interviewed, interspersed with scenes of Prefontaine's life.

In the movie, "Steve Prefontaine" is portrayed by Jared Leto, in his third film, two years after his breakthrough role in the *My So-Called Life* TV series; UO coach "Bill Bowerman" is played by U.S. Marine Corps staff sergeant veteran and Golden Globe–nominated actor R. Lee Ermey; UO coach "Bill Dellinger" is portrayed by TV sitcom *Married...with Children* Golden Globe–nominated actor Ed O'Neill; and Prefontaine's last girlfriend, "Nancy Alleman," is played by Amy Locane, best known then as Sandy Louise Harling on the TV show *Melrose Place*.

In addition to Hollister as technical advisor, UCLA women's cross-country head coach and women's track assistant coach Eric Peterson as running trainer for Leto, and U.S. Olympic Team and University of Washington field coach Ken Shannon as discus trainer for UO teammate "Mac Wilkins" actor Brian McGovern, credited consultants included Dellinger, former girlfriend Elaine Finley Giannone, sister Linda Prefontaine, longtime friend Jim Seyler, former girlfriend Nancy (Alleman) Stanwood, former UO teammate and roommate Pat Tyson, and Wilkins.

On the set of the movie *Prefontaine, from left,* father Raymond Prefontaine, actor Jared Leto, and mother Elfriede Prefontaine. *Courtesy Linda Prefontaine/Prefontaine Productions LLC.*

Despite not agreeing with all of the film portrayals, Tyson nevertheless appreciated the time and effort the actors devoted to put cinematic life into those he knew.

"I think Jared Leto did a good job. But, you know, he has the voice based on a script and a director that doesn't really know Steve. Geoff Hollister and I were there to do our best to try and help out, but Leto's Leto. He worked really, really hard on being Steve—he listened to his voice on radio episodes, on TV episodes, on interviews; watched all the races; tried to create the same flair. And I thought that Jared did a really, really, really good job with the running—and he was not a runner," says Tyson. "I thought with Bowerman, the actor from *Full Metal Jacket,* captured him really well. Lee Ermey was also a military officer—he was in the marines and Bowerman was in the army—but he captured him really, really well."

Tyson also was represented in the movie, portrayed by actor Breckin Meyer, known best then as Travis Birkenstock in the Alicia Silverstone 1995 comedy film *Clueless.*

"We actually had real clothing that I wore that my character played. He wore my college ring, my shorts. He got nervous when I was on set, which made me feel good because if an actor gets nervous that must mean I must be important, too, or something," he says with a laugh. "But he was a little worried that he wasn't going to be able to portray me the way he thought I wanted him to portray me, I guess."

Shooting took place in July and August 1996.

"I was invited all eight weeks just to be there to give any comments that might help. They invited Dellinger on, they invited Linda, and Linda's mom and dad," Tyson recalls. "The guy that played [U.S. Olympian] Gerry Lindgren was a runner that I knew that ran at Arkansas and Oregon. We had a lot of characters that were college runners that I knew that ran in Oregon or Washington, and we had the [Spokane, Washington] Mead High School kids in there, too, so we tried to make that running as accurate as possible."

Having so many people on the set as advisors, consultants, or athletes in acting roles also afforded filmmakers the ability to change course whenever the script or story was altered during filming.

"It was originally going in a different direction and then the cool thing was that the co-writer and director, Steve James, was great interviewing and talking and wanting accuracy," says Tyson. "During the whole time on the movie set the goal was to make it as authentic as possible. That's why they let so many characters in to be part of it to try to authenticate it."

The attempt that was made and how much they paid attention to details to make it as accurate as possible impressed Tyson.

"They were very inviting and actually wanted me there, and they wanted Geoff Hollister there and the others. They just wanted to do it right for the family. It wasn't a perfect deal and it wasn't a big budget either, but they did try," he says. "When I was first with [screenwriter] Gene Corr, he took me to Eugene and he wanted me to take him all over—to the trailer area where we lived; we went to the restaurants; we went to Dellinger's house. What we tried to do was to relive everything so he could smell it and taste it and feel it so when he got to writing he could feel it better. We did that for two days. They really, really made the effort."

Still, Tyson felt Leto's version of Prefontaine missed some of the lighter qualities he also possessed.

"I think the script made him a little more intense; Pre was more relaxed. The script's going to maybe change that a little bit, like [Leto's Prefontaine saying] 'I'm not a runner.' I don't think Pre ever looked at himself not as a runner; I think he always knew he was a runner. But they kind of played that in there to create a little more energy, a little excitement because it's a hard story to tell in a Hollywood picture," Tyson observes.

The majority of the locations were shot in Tyson's home state of Washington, including Marysville, Olympia, Seattle, Snohomish, Stanwood, and Tacoma.

"They couldn't use the real Eugene, Oregon because [filming rights] were already bought out by the *Without Limits* group, so they said we can still do this and we'll do it in Seattle. So they got a little home that looked a little bit like Coos Bay and they did a nice set along the water and a home that looked a lot like Elrod Street there in Coos Bay where Steve grew up," he says of Olympia.

In addition to the use of original 1972 Munich Olympic Summer Games footage from the Disney-owned ABC-TV coverage, some of the sites filmed included Buckaroo Tavern, 4021 Fremont Avenue North, Seattle; Discovery Park, 3801 Discovery Park Boulevard, Seattle; Baker Stadium (for Hayward Field) at the University of Puget Sound, 1500 North Warner Street, Tacoma; and Husky Stadium (for Munich Olympic Stadium) at the University of Washington, Montlake Boulevard, Seattle.

"They were able to take the University of Puget Sound and make it a Hayward Field—even though it was a black track, but we couldn't do too much about that. But they did everything else to make Hayward look pretty accurate. They went over and created a beautiful setting that looked like it was Bill Bowerman's house overlooking the McKenzie River [in Oregon], but they did it north of Seattle in a place called Snohomish, Washington," Tyson explains. "And Munich was the University of Washington and the dorms were where the athletes would be living, and the terrorist episode was pretty accurate in every way. So all the details relating to the sets were really, really good."

During the time he spent on the movie set, Tyson also quickly realized the challenges between capturing real life and movie life.

"For the trailer scenes, I told them to don't mess it up, make it perfect in there because Steve liked it clean. But they messed it up because that wasn't good for Hollywood because they wanted to make it look a little busy in there. One of those Hollywood things," said Tyson, who knew of what he spoke because the trailer in which he and Prefontaine lived was indeed clean and neat. "But I would say that it was 80 percent accurate, but they had to kind of speed things up because they only had about one hundred minutes or so."

*Prefontaine* was one of the films shown at the 1997 Sundance Film Festival in Utah, one of the nation's largest and most respected independent film festivals.

On location during filming of the movie *Without Limits*, which starred Billy Crudup as Steve Prefontaine. *Photos by Steve Bence.*

The following year, in 1998, the $25 million budget *Without Limits* was released. Directed by Towne and co-written by Towne and Moore, the 118-minute film is a more traditional narrative, and to tell the story, it focuses primarily on Prefontaine, Bowerman, and Prefontaine's penultimate girlfriend, Mary Marckx.

In this movie, "Steve Prefontaine" is played by Billy Crudup, an award-winning stage actor six movies into his film career. "Bill Bowerman" is portrayed by Golden Globe and Emmy Award–winning actor Donald Sutherland, who twenty years earlier was professor Dave Jennings in *National Lampoon's Animal House*, filmed at UO. "Bill Dellinger" is played by longtime character actor Dean Norris (twenty years before his *Breaking Bad* role). And "Mary Marckx" is portrayed by Monica Potter, who the previous year in *Con Air* played the wife of Nicolas Cage's character.

Athletes in acting roles include the likes of U.S. Olympian Jeff Atkinson as UO teammate "Steve Bence," two-time U.S. Olympic Marathon medalist Frank Shorter as Olympic announcer "Fred Long," two-time U.S. Olympian Pat Porter as Finnish Olympian "Lasse Viren," and University of Portland athlete Garth Granholm as U.S. Olympian "George Young."

"Crudup worked hard to copy Pre in mannerism and the way he ran. He did a great job," opined Bence, who saw that aspect firsthand by Prefontaine himself—and by Crudup in filmed scenes such as when the actor high-fived fans at Hayward Field. "[Seeing] Billy Crudup slapping hands with the fans after his three-mile at the University of Oregon; Pre endeared himself to 'Pre's People' with a gutsy run-from-the-front effort. Regarding Jeff Atkinson playing me, only one line made it into the movie. Atkinson ran in the Seoul 1988 Olympics and missed making the 1996 Atlanta Olympics. He went to Eugene to participate in the movie and got the role of playing me. He's a much better runner than actor."

There were plenty of experts to help ensure accuracy and details during filming. In addition to Bence, among them were technical advisor and track and field trainer Patrice "Pat" Donnelly, the U.S. Olympic hurdler who was also an actor and technical advisor on *Personal Best*; Bill and Barbara Bowerman; UO president Dave Frohnmayer; Jim Jaqua, son of John Jaqua, who helped Bowerman and Phil Knight create Blue Ribbon Sports (Nike); Mary Marckx Creel; and Moore, who also served as an executive producer.

"I'm credited as the track and field consultant," said Bence. "I contributed by loaning my clothing—uniforms, sweats, T-shirts, etc. from that time—and my training journals. I gave input to the scriptwriting, was on the set for a lot of the filming, and generated support from true fans of the era. Kenny Moore called me out of the blue to work on the movie. [He is] a great writer who knew Pre well [and] wrote the first major drafts and wanted Mary Marckx and I to consult, which we did. There was some tension [between Towne and Marckx] between being completely accurate and writing an entertaining two-hour movie. I [recall] a two-hour meeting that Crudup had with Marckx and I. He was dressed in character, and it felt as though we were talking to Pre, twenty years after his death."

On-location filming in Oregon included Coos Bay; Cottage Grove; Eugene; Heceta Beach, Florence; and Springfield. And Citrus Community College, 1000 West Foothill Boulevard, Glendora, California, was used to replicate some Olympic footage that supplemented real 1972 Munich Olympic Summer Games footage from the Warner Bros.-owned *Visons of Eight* Olympic Games documentary.

According to UO, among the scenes filmed on campus were shot at Gerlinger Pool, Hayward Field, Hendricks Hall, McArthur Court, University Inn, and University Street.

And Bowerman himself allowed scenes to be filmed at his McKenzie View Drive house in Eugene, which overlooks the McKenzie River.

At the end of the movie credits, it states, "This film is based on the life of Steve Prefontaine. Dialogue and certain events and characters contained in the film were created for the purpose of dramatization."

Story changes in movies are made for brevity, film time, pace, drama—all sorts of reasons, to varying degrees of logic. For example, when Prefontaine won the 1970 NCAA Outdoor Track and Field Championships in Des Moines, Iowa, he did so a few days after he cut open his foot on a diving board bolt at the team's motel swimming pool, which required several stitches. In the film, however, he cuts his foot during an escapade in the bedroom. Another instance is with Prefontaine's freshman 1970 two-mile 8:40.0 win against Stanford University and Fresno State College (California State University–Fresno) at Fresno, California, and his three-mile 13:12.8 win versus Washington State University (WSU) at Hayward Field.

"The movie compressed two races from Pre's freshman years—the March 21 Stanford meet and his April 25 race in 13:12.8 against WSU—so it appears that his first three-mile race at Oregon was against Stanford's Don Kardong," Bence pointed out.

"But Robert Towne won over the trust of Bowerman and spent hours interviewing Bill and rewriting the script," Bence added. "The movie went from being a story of Prefontaine to the realistic relationship between Bowerman and Pre."

For his performance, Sutherland was nominated for a Golden Globe Award for Best Supporting Actor in a Motion Picture. He was also runner-up for a National Society of Film Critics Award for Best Supporting Actor and won the International Press Academy Satellite Award for Best Supporting Actor in a Motion Picture—Drama.

*Chapter 7*

# OUTSIDE OREGON:

# HIGH SCHOOL, COLLEGE,

# INTERNATIONAL...

There were many places where Steve Prefontaine competed, resided, visited, made public appearances, volunteered, and worked. He was well traveled, whether statewide, nationwide, or worldwide. While too numerous to mention in detail, there are many, for various reasons, worth noting.

In his 1969 outdoor season, the eighteen-year-old senior competed in the Golden West Invitational at Sacramento City College's Hughes Stadium, 3835 Freeport Boulevard in Sacramento, California, where he won the mile (4:06.0); AAU Outdoor Track and Field Championships at Dade County Junior College (Miami Dade College), 300 Northeast 2nd Avenue in Miami, Florida, where his fourth-place 13:43.0 in the three-mile was high school's third all-time; and the Hawaii Invitational at Punahou School's Alexander Field, 1601 Punahou Street in Honolulu, Hawaii, where he was second in the two-mile (8:48.8).

It was at the 1969 AAUs in Miami where newly crowned 1969 NCAA three-mile champion Frank Shorter first met Prefontaine.

"Kenny Moore knew Steve Prefontaine, and I met him there after the race," noted Shorter of his fellow USA National Team running mates. "When we got on the team to go to Europe, it was a traveling U.S. track and field team, and Steve and Kenny and I roomed together. That's where we got to know each other, in the summer of 1969."

Portland, Oregon signpost at Pioneer Courthouse Square. *Photo by Paul Clerici.*

After the first competition in America—the U.S.-USSR-British Commonwealth meet on July 19 at the Los Angeles Coliseum at Exposition Park, 700 Exposition Park Drive in Los Angeles, California, where Prefontaine was fifth in the 5,000 meters (14:40.0)—the team traveled overseas for a series of international meets.

First up for the American squad was the U.S.-Europe meet on July 31, 1969, in Stuttgart, West Germany. In the 5,000 meters, Prefontaine's third-place 13:52.8 placed him second on the all-time high school standings. Five days later, on August 5 in Augsburg, West Germany, at the U.S.-West Germany meet, Prefontaine was edged out by 4.6 seconds in the 5,000 meters for second place (14:07.4). And at the U.S.-Great Britain meet in London, England, on August 13, Prefontaine ended his high school years with a fourth-place 14:38.4 in the 5,000 meters.

"What we also found out on that trip was our training was so similar," Shorter pointed out. "It was the most similar to any other runner I'd met up until that point in training because Jack Bacheler was a little bit slower on his intervals—he did a few more—and I trained like a 5,000-meter racer. That's just what I developed being my own coach. Even my coach at Yale said, 'By your middle of your junior year you were making up your own workouts. You were coaching yourself.' I'd been doing that and that's what I'd settled on, and I was formulating my own way. We essentially ran very fast for no more than three miles worth of intervals at a time at 5K race pace. The other workout that we would do, when an important race was coming up—and it was just coincidental—was a stepdown workout where you would run a mile, three-quarter, two halves, and two or four quarters. I'll never forget in Augsburg we ran that workout the Tuesday before he ran on a weekend, and it was all in faster than 65 seconds a quarter. It was just a tune-up. You take a little more rest so you don't get tired, but it shows you you're in shape. It shows you you're ready. It's different from the other workouts that you do and it's easier to do well because you're getting the rest, so it's not an all-out effort."

In Prefontaine's 1969-70 freshman year at the University of Oregon (UO), he went out fast. As a frosh Duck, he made *Track & Field News* with a November 1969 full-frame cover photo from his victorious NCAA District 8 Northern Division Cross-Country Championship six-mile at Oregon State University (OSU) in Avery Park, Southwest Avery Park Drive in Corvallis, Oregon. Based in part on UO's tactical decision to wear spikes for the wet and muddy course, Prefontaine defeated the flats-wearing twenty-three-year-old U.S. Olympian Gerry Lindgren (2nd, 29:41) by 27.2 seconds in his first competitive six-miler. UO's 19-44 win over Washington State University (WSU) was led by Prefontaine in first (29:13.8).

Later that month, on November 15, Prefontaine turned in one of his most exciting finishes in his young career—and lost! At Stanford Golf Course at 91 Links Road in Stanford, California, the 1969 Pac-8 Conference Cross-Country Championship 5.9 mile was hosted by Stanford University. Prefontaine and Lindgren elbowed and nudged each other en route to a simultaneous 28:32.4 finish, where Lindgren's lean prevailed for the victory. And on November 24, at the 1969 NCAA Cross-Country Championship six-mile at Van Cortlandt Park in the Bronx, New York, Prefontaine came in third (29:12.0).

Much like he did in cross-country, Prefontaine took charge in his first collegiate indoor track season as well. On the heels of reportedly suffering from the flu the previous week, he won the 1970 Oregon Invitational indoor two-mile in Portland, Oregon, with a PR 8:39.2 via miles of 4:21 and 4:18.2 on the eleven-lap wood track. This took place inside the then-ten-year-old Memorial Coliseum at 300 North Winning Way.

In the 1970 outdoor track season, Prefontaine went a combined 11-0 in March, April, and May, which included the Pac-8 Northern Division three-mile title (13:32.0) on May 9 in Seattle, Washington, and the Pac-8 Championship three-mile title (13:27.8) on May 16 in Los Angeles, California. He also recorded PRs in the mile in 4:00.4 (versus OSU on May 2); two-mile in 8:40.0 (against Fresno State College/Stanford University in Fresno, California, on March 21); and three-mile in 13:12.8 (versus WSU on April 25), which regained him the year's top three-mile spot and landed him at number seven all-time in the United States.

On June 20, at the 1970 NCAA Outdoor Track and Field Championships in Des Moines, Iowa, on a bandaged and stitched-up foot a few days after cutting it open on a jagged bolt at a swimming pool, he turned in a 13:22.0 winning three-mile. And the following week, at the 1970 AAU Outdoor Track and Field Championships in Bakersfield, California, another stellar three-mile was contested with Prefontaine in fifth (13:26.0).

Once again representing the United States, Prefontaine in July 1970 traveled to Europe for another series of international competitions. At the U.S.-West Germany meet in Stuttgart, West Germany, Prefontaine in the 5,000 meters finished second (13:39.6). In Leningrad at the U.S.-USSR meet in the Soviet Union, Prefontaine was again the runner-up in the 5,000 meters (13:49.4). And in an international meet in Moscow, he won the 1,500 meters in 3:44.9.

In November 1970, his undefeated sophomore cross-country season included the Pac-8 Northern Division Cross-Country title in Pullman, Washington (30:11.8), and his first NCAA cross-county title, in Williamsburg, Virginia, in a record 28:00.2 over the six-mile course (the meet distance changed to 10,000 meters in 1976).

In indoor track at the 1971 Oregon Invitational in February in Portland, Prefontaine won the two-mile in 8:31.6. And in a span of three weeks, he landed atop the U.S. rankings in the two-mile on March 20 at a quad-meet in Eugene (8:33.2), the mile on March 27 at San Diego State University (4:00.2), and the three-mile on April 3 versus Stanford University (13:01.6). He closed out the regular season undefeated in the mile (PR 3:59.1), two-mile (PR 8:33.2), and three-mile (PR 13:01.6).

He began the postseason with wins in the 1971 Pac-8 Northern Division two-mile (8:42.4) in Pullman and the 1971 Pac-8 Conference Championship mile (4:01.5) and three-mile (13:18.0) in Seattle. In June, after a runner-up 3:57.4 in the Oregon Twilight Meet mile in Eugene, Prefontaine won the 1971 NCAA Championship three-mile heat (13:34.6) and final (13:20.2) in Seattle and the 1971 AAU Championship three-mile (12:58.6) in Eugene, which put him at number five all-time and the number-two American.

Steve Prefontaine at the 1971 U.S.-USSR All-Stars Meet in Berkeley, California. *University Archives photograph, UA Ref3, University of Oregon Libraries Special Collections and University Archives UA_REF_3_A_ATHPRE0004rb.*

He closed out the season in July with another set of summertime international competitions—on American tracks this time—with an AR 13:30.4 in the 5,000 meters at the U.S.-USSR-World All-Stars meet at the University of California–Berkeley; and a 13:57.6 winning 5,000 meters at the U.S.-Africa meet in Durham, North Carolina, before heading off to the Pan American Games (interestingly, the day after his U.S.-Africa win, Prefontaine utilized his UO broadcast communication major and contributed on-air television commentary for the 10,000-meter race). At the 1971 Pan American Games, in Cali, Colombia, Prefontaine won 5,000-meter gold in 13:52.53 on August 2, just over four months after the outdoor season began.

His undefeated junior cross-country season culminated in the postseason with his third Pac-8 Northern Division six-mile title (28:10.8) in Eugene; and the Pac-8 Conference Championships at a University of California–Los Angeles (UCLA) course reportedly at six miles, 410 yards, which Prefontaine won in a CR 29:59.6.

On November 22, at the 1971 NCAA Cross-Country Championships in Knoxville, Tennessee, only at his insistence did the harrier team of Randall James, Michael Long, Richard Ritchie, Mark Savage, and Pat Tyson compete after UO reportedly initially said it would send only Prefontaine to defend his title. As a result, Prefontaine (29:18.0) and UO (83 points to second-place WSU's 122) won, for UO coach Bill Dellinger's first cross-country title.

The Olympic year of 1972 began for Prefontaine with a college-record 8:26.6 indoor two-mile in Portland, Oregon, on January 28, as the second-fastest American; and, in front of over sixteen thousand in the stands, another 8:26.6 winning two-mile at the 1972 *Los Angeles Times* Indoor Track Games inside The Forum, 3900 West Manchester Boulevard, in Inglewood, California, on February 11.

An undefeated 1972 outdoor track season was the prelude to the Olympics, as Prefontaine turned in regular-season PRs of 3:39.8 in the 1,500 meters (May 6 versus OSU), 3:56.7 in the mile as the tenth fastest in the nation (April 23 at the Oregon Twilight Meet in Eugene), 8:35.2 in the two-mile (April 15 at the University of Nebraska in Lincoln), and an AR 13:29.6 in the 5,000 meters (April 29 versus WSU).

He capped it off with the Pac-8 Conference Championship three-mile title (13:32.2) on May 20 at Stanford University; 1972 NCAA Outdoor Track and Field Championship 5,000-meter title (MR 13:31.4), after he also won his heat in 14:01.4, at UO; and the Rose Festival Track and Field Meet at Mount Hood Community College, 26000 Southeast Start Street, in Gresham, Oregon, where his final pre-Olympic Trials tune-up was a top college AR time of 7:45.8 in the 3,000 meters.

In July 1972, the U.S. Olympic Track and Field Team spent about two weeks at a training camp designed by the U.S. Olympic Committee and housed at Bowdoin College, 255 Main Street, in Brunswick, Maine.

"I have a Maine postcard Steve sent me, showing the coast and the ruggedness," says Tyson. "And on the postcard, he mentioned that 'You would love it here because it is so much like the Oregon coast that it makes me feel like I'm at home.' The salt water, the seagulls—it's just who you are, and Pre was a man of the Oregon coast."

Team USA, which included among them U.S. Olympic coaches Bill Bowerman and Dellinger, then made its way to New York and flew to Norway for some pre-Olympic competition tune-ups. They stayed at the Panorama Sommerhotell in Oslo, Norway and trained mostly at the Sports and Physical Education College of Norway.

At the original Bislett Stadium (replaced in 2005 by a new Bislett Stadium at Louises gate 1, 0168 Oslo, Norway), Prefontaine in the 1,500 meters was second (3:39.4). The following day, he set an AR 7:44.2 in the Oslo 3,000 meters versus a stellar field that included fellow Americans Doug Brown, Jeff Galloway, Glen Hilton, and Shorter; Mariano Haro Cisneros of Spain; Francesco "Franco" Arese of Italy; Per Halle of Norway; and New Zealanders Rod Dixon, Dick Quax, and Richard Taylor, among the field of seventeen starters.

"The very first meeting I had with Steve Prefontaine," recalled Dixon, "it was in Oslo, Norway, in 1972, which was one of the meetings as a buildup towards the Olympic Games. I had run the 1,500 meters the day before, and I ran the 3,000 meters [in which] he virtually ran away from some of the best distance runners in the world, setting a new AR and fastest time for the year. That's when I knew that he was going to be a factor in the 5,000 meters in Munich."

Shorter recalled that the American contingent left Norway by charter and arrived in Munich on August 19, early enough to settle in before their various events. "A lot of us had significant others who came over, so it was not like [being in] isolation. So you felt really at home; you'd been there a while. We lived in the Village the whole time and even had enough time to have a practice meet before the Games started," Shorter noted of the meet in which Prefontaine won a 3,000-meter race on August 24 and continued a farther 218.69 meters for an AR two-mile 8:19.4, thanks to Bowerman and Dellinger, who premeasured the added distance to meet both marks.

Olympic Stadium in Munich, Germany. *Courtesy Munich Olympic Park.*

The Games of the XX Olympiad played out from August 26 to September 11, in Munich, Germany, some 360 miles south of Berlin. It held special meaning for Prefontaine (who was part German from his Germany-born mother) and Shorter (born in Munich while his U.S. Army physician father was stationed there in 1947). To relax and enjoy the area, athletes visited sites such as Marienplatz, the Rathaus-Glockenspiel clock, New Town Hall, and other places of interest.

"Yeah, we visited touristy things," said Shorter, who added with a chuckle, "and one of the most interesting things I remember was right near the entrance to the Olympic Village. They'd made a big hill, an artificial hill, and what they'd done is cover over an old huge garbage dump. That was a dump! But it was no trouble getting around the city. We had a pass for the subway, and we could go anywhere."

All that time spent together—training, competing, traveling—fostered natural camaraderie between the athletes.

"[In the Athletes Village,] we had a room where everybody in that room was part of different enclaves; it was really a combination of the Florida Track Club and Oregon Track Club enclaves in the room. And the exception was Dave Wottle [Bowling Green State University]; he was my roommate," noted Shorter.

Two days before Prefontaine's 5,000-meter heat, on September 5, Palestinian Liberation Organization (PLO) Black September terrorists entered Athletes Village Building #31, which housed the team from Israel. They killed a coach and an athlete and by gunpoint held hostage several more Israeli athletes and officials. Less than twenty-four hours later, after a failed attempted rescue and a shootout at the nearby Fürstenfeldbruck Air Base, where the terrorists and hostages had been bused, seventeen people in total were dead (four coaches, two officials, and five athletes, all from the Israeli team; one police officer; and five terrorists).

In the days leading up to the tragedy, every effort had been made to present a peaceful, friendly Olympics, which did include an observed lack of security not seen in previous Games.

"You got the feeling that the German people were really trying to show that it was no longer Nazi Germany. They really were. Which made the massacre that much more painful," Shorter pointed out. "Because if you think about it, they probably were erring on the side of when security came [in the early days], they were always worried more about the appearance of the security, and they didn't want to look like Nazi German soldiers in hobnail boots."

After they were initially instructed to remain in their rooms for safety, athletes, coaches, and officials dealt with the aftereffects in many different ways, from continuing their regular schedules and patterns to wanting to leave. On September 6, Dellinger had taken Prefontaine to nearby Austria to clear his head and separate himself from the wake of the terror.

The Games resumed after a thirty-four-hour period of mourning, which included a memorial service. For Prefontaine, that meant finally realizing his dream in front of eighty thousand spectators inside Olympiastadion (Olympic Stadium) at Spiridon-Louis-Ring 27, 80809, Munich.

Five separate 5,000-meter heats were run on September 7. In his heat, Prefontaine was second (13:32.6). Of the sixty-one qualifiers who would compete in the finals, Prefontaine recorded the second-fastest time overall.

The 5,000-meter final was held three days later, on September 10, with a stacked field that included among them Mohamed Gammoudi of Tunisia, Emiel Puttemans of Belgium, Ian Stewart of Great Britain, and Lasse Viren of Finland.

After numerous laps of jostling and maneuvering, and the leaders with a 4:30 first mile and 4:26.4 second mile (8:56.4), Prefontaine in typical fashion led, with laps of 62.5 and 61.2. He was then passed by Viren and Puttemans but then regained the lead on a 60.3 lap with about 600 meters remaining. Over the final lap, both Viren and Gammoudi passed Prefontaine, in third with close to 250 meters left.

In the mad muscle-burning rush to the finish line, Viren won gold (13:26.4) and Gammoudi silver (13:27.4). Nearing bronze, Prefontaine on spent legs sputtered to the line as a stronger-legged Stewart confidently grabbed third (13:27.6), just eight-tenths ahead of fourth-placed Prefontaine (13:28.4), who turned in a 4:04 final mile.

"I was one of the few people who could tell him he'd run a stupid race," noted Shorter. "You don't run in the outside lane around the final turn. And he'd also told people that he was going to run the last four laps under four minutes. Ian Stewart said, 'Hell, four of us can do that.' And he telegraphed what he was going to do, and he did it, which was nuts."

Prefontaine did indeed boast prior to the Games that he could run that last mile fast, but that did not intimidate the Europeans. As 1968 U.S. Olympian Marty Liquori also recalled, "Here's what Ian Stewart told me: 'Prefontaine says he will run the last mile in four minutes. So what! We can all do that. He has no kick.'"

Prefontaine was reportedly so down about his non-medal Olympic performance that many recall he was thinking about not competing for a long while. However true were his words—whether he was simply vocally exorcising the demons or if it was an actual possibility—before he returned home Prefontaine ran the Zauli Memorial 5,000 meters in Rome, Italy, on September 13, with an AR 13:26.4 second-place finish; and the Coca-Cola Invitational two-mile at Crystal Palace in London, England, on September 15, with another runner-up spot (8:24.8).

John Kaegi, Prefontaine's UO fraternity brother and friend, received mail that contained that very post-Olympic concern.

"He wrote to me on his way home that he was discouraged and embarrassed and that he was quitting competitive track," he said. "I responded with encouragement and positivity, but he fell into a dark place for a few months until he read that Lasse Viren would be running in the [1973 Sunkist Invitational Indoor Track and Field Meet]. Steve got a wildcard entry to the race at the last minute and only trained for a couple of weeks, yet he [beat] Viren on his way to victory in that race, which rekindled his desire and commitment to track."

The 1973 indoor track season took Prefontaine outside Oregon. At that season-opening Sunkist Invitational inside Los Angeles Arena in California, he began the year on January 20 with an 8:27.4 two-mile win over runner-up Liquori in 8:38.8 (Viren was sixth, 8:49.0).

Two days after he turned twenty-two, at the Oregon Invitational in Portland on January 27, Prefontaine clocked an AR-winning 8:24.6 in the two-mile. And on February 9, he ran the mile at the 1973 *Los Angeles Times* Indoor Games at The Forum in Inglewood, California, with the year's first sub-4:00 mile, winning in 3:59.2 ahead of runner-up Gianni del Buono of Italy and Liquori in third.

"I don't remember the first time I met Prefontaine—I was an East Coast guy, he was a West Coast guy, [and] we were in different events," said Liquori. "As of the race at the *LA Times*, I knew I had run two races that weekend.… On Friday night I ran against Pre. My diary says Pre led from the second lap on and I felt good. With two laps to go, I thought I had him, and then he pulled away."

After what Prefontaine would describe as a period of rest, which still included weeks of seventy to ninety miles to help reduce injuries he was experiencing, the UO senior at this point turned it up a bit to continue his running regime. His two-mile indoor slate was impressive, as he went 7-1 and recorded four of the top six sub-8:30 American times.

During his undefeated 1973 collegiate outdoor track season, away meets included an AR 27:09.4 six-mile at the Bakersfield All-Comers Meet in

Bakersfield, California, on March 24; and a 13:27.2 three-mile against OSU at Corvallis, Oregon, on May 5.

In Baton Rouge, Louisiana, at the 1973 NCAA Outdoor Track and Field Championships, in the three-mile Prefontaine won his preliminary heat (MR 13:19.0). Two days later, on June 9, he won his record-setting fourth consecutive outdoor title with a 13:05.3. He then followed up with his final collegiate track meet at the 1973 AAU Outdoor Track and Field Championships, in Bakersfield, where he won his three-mile heat (13:17.8) on June 14 and then on June 16 the final in a world's sixth-best 12:53.4.

Three days after he competed in the first Hayward Field Restoration Meet at UO, Prefontaine embarked for Europe to run in a series of meets in Finland (Helsinki, Kajaani, Joensuu, Oulu), West Germany (Munich), and Belgium (Louvain) during the summer months of June and July 1973. He realized the advantages of competing internationally against the same athletes he could face in other meets leading up to the Olympics.

In three races in the Finnish capital, he ran a third-place 3:43.1 in the 1,500 meters at the Helsinki International Meet on June 23. And then in two consecutive days at the World Games inside Helsinki Olympic Stadium—built for the 1952 Helsinki Summer Olympic Games, 1 Paavo Nurmi Road—he turned in a runner-up AR 13:22.4 in the 5,000 meters to Puttemans (13:19.6) on June 27, with Viren in fifth; and in a 1,500-meter field of nearly a dozen record-setting runners, he finished eleventh with an Oregon state collegiate PR 3:38.1 on June 28.

In July, Prefontaine wound up his series with five races in three countries within fifteen days.

In non-AAU meets in Finland, he was second in the Kajaani International Meet 1,500 meters (3:46.5); third in the Joensuu International Meet 1,500 meters (3:48.2); first in the Oulu International Meet 5,000 meters (13:40.6); runner-up in the U.S.-West Germany-Sweden Meet 5,000 meters (13:23.8) in Munich, Germany; and second in the Louvain International Meet 5,000 meters (13:35.2) in Belgium—but ahead of third-place Viren (14:09.6)—as his back was again acting up.

On Labor Day weekend in 1973, Prefontaine was invited to speak, greet runners, and help present awards at the inaugural Charleston Distance Run in West Virginia. Race director Don Cohen, in an attempt to generate interest in his no-fee fifteen-miler during the nascent days of the running boom, created a Hall of Fame and also invited the likes of legendary four-time 1936 U.S. Olympic gold medalist Jesse Owens.

Steve Prefontaine, *left*, with U.S. Olympian Jesse Owens. *Courtesy The Ohio State University Archives.*

*From left*: Charleston Distance Run race director Don Cohen, Dave Wottle, Jeff Galloway, Steve Prefontaine, and Jacqueline Hansen. *Courtesy Jacqueline Hansen.*

Prefontaine was extremely popular as a guest speaker, no matter the age of the audience.

"I had him do three junior high assemblies, and one of them had about seven hundred kids in the audience," recalls Tyson of a time Prefontaine spoke at his Washington school. "No principal's going to allow a guest speaker to come in and talk to junior high kids for an hour because it ain't gonna work. But guess what? It worked with Pre. They listened, they were enamored, and when he was finished, they all wanted his autograph—all seven hundred of them! They almost mobbed him! His message was exercise and eating right and anti-drug and loving life and finding your passion. He talked for an hour! He could present it. And seven hundred kids were spellbound. He did two or three of those that weekend."

In his final collegiate cross-country, delayed from when he skipped the post-Olympic 1972 harrier season, one of the matches was a 3-point 26-29 UO win over Prefontaine's future Oregon Track Club, in which he won the 6.28-miler in 29:44. He also won the 1973 Pac-8 Conference Northern Division title; Pac-8 Conference Cross-Country Championship 5.9-mile title (CR 28:05.4) at Stanford University Golf Course; and the 1973 Oregon state cross-country title at Tokatee Golf Club, 54947 McKenzie Highway, in Blue River, Oregon.

November 19 was the 1973 NCAA Cross-Country Championships at Hangman Valley Golf Course, 2210 East Hangman Valley Road, at WSU in Spokane, Washington. Prefontaine battled his sore back and a talented field that included Western Kentucky University's Nick Rose of Bristol, England, the 1971 International Junior Cross-Country winner; East Tennessee State University's Neil Cusack of Ireland, the defending champion; and Craig Virgin, who broke Prefontaine's two-mile AR with an 8:40.9 in 1973, among them.

For a good portion of the six-mile course, in front of an estimated four thousand lining the route, Rose held the lead over Prefontaine, who in his final Duck meet eventually clawed back and earned a hard-fought 28:14.8 victory for his third title (1970, 1971, 1973) in four years as only the second collegian to do so at the time.

Prefontaine's first post-collegiate competitions were in the 1974 indoor track season.

On January 11, at the CYO Invitational Indoor Track Meet at Cole Field House, 4095 Union Lane, in College Park, Maryland, he suffered his first loss to a countryman in a race over a mile since 1970, when Dick Buerkle won the two-mile in 8:26.2, seven seconds ahead of his 8:33.2.

He followed up the loss with an 8:33.0 two-mile win at the 1974 Sunkist Invitational Indoor Track and Field Meet in Los Angeles, California. He then set an AR 8:22.2 two-mile win at the Oregon Invitational in Portland, before another rare loss at the 1974 *Los Angeles Times* Indoor Track Games, inside The Forum in Inglewood, California, where he came in second (3:59.5) to Tony Waldrop's 3:58.3.

Prefontaine closed out indoors on February 17 at the San Diego Indoor Track Meet with an AR and world third-fastest-two-mile 8:20.4 win.

After a handful of outdoor track meets between April and June 1974—which included a world sixth-best and AR 27:43.6 at the Oregon Twilight Meet 10,000 meters on April 27 and, six weeks later, a world third-best and AR 12:51.4 three-mile at the 1974 Hayward Restoration Meet at UO—Prefontaine continued his stand against the AAU and decided to compete in Europe instead of AAU's own self-appointed showcase.

This took him in June and July 1974 to international meets in Finland—Tampere 3,000-meter (1st, 7:55.8), Kauhava 3,000-meter (1st, 8:00.4), Saarijärvi 3,000-meter (1st, 8:07.4), Helsinki World Games 5,000-meter (2nd, AR/PR 13:21.9), Varkaus 3,000-meter (1st, 7:57.4), and Joutseno

5,000-meter (1$^{st}$, 13:55.6); Italy—Milan 3,000-meter (2$^{nd}$, AR 7:42.6); and Sweden—Stockholm July Games two-mile (3$^{rd}$, 8:18.4).

Within the first seven months of 1974, Prefontaine set nine ARs in an unprecedented stretch of excellence, thus owning all ARs from 3,000 meters to 10,000 meters!

UO Duck Steve Bence recalled these were still trying times due to the AAU, which threatened to ban/suspend athletes who refused to compete in its own U.S. meets and/or who ran overseas during AAU-designated moratorium periods.

"The AAU prohibited track athletes from competing internationally during certain dates of the summer in an effort to force U.S. athletes to compete in its own meets, the AAU championships, and the meet against the USSR," he said. "Not only did Pre plan to skip the AAU championships, he told the world he was skipping them. Pre encouraged many of us to join him in Europe for the summer, assuring that we could show up, enter meets just as he had done the year before, and get paid. The AAU offered no help with his [or others'] costs of training, competition, and living. He was internationally famous—a reputation he solidified in college—but frustrated; all but forced to take race money under the table."

But that they did.

"I was intrigued by the idea of extending my junior 800-meter season and having a European summer adventure," Bence noted. "I, along with seven or eight others, took Pre up on the offer. I spent nearly two months hopping through Norway, Sweden, and Finland, negotiating payment with meet directors, running sixteen races, and pocketing the money. After expenses, I made $133. I broke the rules, both of the NCAA and the AAU, which I've never regretted. I had reasons to do it that I think are all the more relevant today. I returned to the U.S. on August 7, exhilarated from my results, but also from joining Pre in his fight. Even though we were technically wrong, I believed that we did the right thing."

Prefontaine returned to Europe in the fall for a pair of meets in Finland and England. This was about a week after his 3:58.3 mile on September 3 in Eugene, when farmers were burning their seed fields and heavy smoke traveled over the track and caused him to cough up blood afterward. Not knowing the extent of damage to which his coughing inflicted, he finished third in the International Meet 5,000 meters (13:27.4) in Helsinki on September 10 and three days later in London failed to finish the only time in his career, when he DNF'd the Coca-Cola two-mile due to later-diagnosed "torn stomach muscles."

In January 1975, over the course of a Texas weekend, Prefontaine was among about two dozen athletes who subjected themselves to myriad physical and mental tests all in the name of science, headed by *Aerobics* author Dr. Kenneth Cooper.

Tests took place at various locations, including the Aerobics Activity Center Clinic and the Institute of Aerobics Research, on Preston Road in Dallas, Texas; Dallas Independent School District's Alfred J. Loos Stadium, 3815 Spring Valley Road, in Addison, Texas; and Willow Bend Polo Club in Plano, Texas (before it moved to Oak Point, Texas).

According to The Cooper Institute website, "Some of the most important testing components included resting heart rate and blood pressure; resting ECG; percent body fat with underwater weighing; measurement of VO2 max with maximal treadmill stress test; measures of running efficiency; lung function testing; biopsy of calf muscle. In summary, this 1975 study found that the elite runners had significantly lower resting heart rates, BMIs, and percent body fat than average men within this age group. The runners also had significantly higher VO2 max, maximal heart rate, left ventricle size, running efficiency, lung function, percent slow twitch fibers, and muscle enzyme activity than average men. These findings gave researchers a much better understanding of how elite distance runners are different from us mere mortals."

Prefontaine possessed a remarkable "84.4 milligrams-per-kilogram of body weight per minute," as well as 77 percent slow-twitch muscle fibers and 210-beats-a-minute heart rate.

In the 1975 indoors, Prefontaine (3:58.6) lost to Liquori (3:57.7) in the mile at the CYO Invitational Indoor Track Meet at Cole Field House in College Park, Maryland, on January 10. A week later, at the Sunkist Invitational Indoor Track and Field Meet inside the Los Angeles Sports Arena at 3939 Figueroa Street (razed in 2016) in Los Angeles, California, he turned in an indoor world seventh-best 8:24.4 two-mile. On January 25, at the Oregon Invitational in Portland, he ran the nation's eighth-fastest two-mile in 8:27.0.

"For the [CYO] race, what I have in my diary is that I ran 3:57.7 and Prefontaine was second in 3:58. I ran 56.8 for the last lap," noted Liquori.

In February, inside The Forum at the 1975 *Los Angeles Times* Indoor Track Games in Inglewood, an admittedly ailing Prefontaine was fifth in the mile (4:03.4) for last place, his worst finish since high school.

The following week, on February 15, he won the two-mile (8:24.4) at the 1975 San Diego Indoor Games at the San Diego Sports Arena (Pechanga Arena), 3500 Sports Arena Boulevard, in San Diego.

Shortly after indoors, Prefontaine joined Shorter for a few weeks to train in Denver, Colorado, and then at about nine thousand feet in Taos, New Mexico, to take advantage of higher altitude.

"We ran there and skied. Ran twice a day, maybe fifteen miles total, and skied downhill in between. I taught him how to ski. First time I took him to ski when we were up in Taos, he never skied before. We got him some rental equipment. I'd showed him how to snowplow, how to turn and stuff. We get off the chairlift, not a very long trail, and he comes over to the start, he starts down the hill and goes straight into the hay bales at the bottom," Shorter said with a hearty laugh. "Probably going twenty-five miles an hour. He got up. By the time we left—we were there about a week—he was skiing. Had him up on the mountain. Natural athlete. And defiant to learn and focused and knowing your body—proprioception."

Back home, the last group of competitions for Prefontaine was six victories between 2,000 and 10,000 meters in April-May 1975. All but one of those races were during a five-meet schedule he organized for invited Finnish athletes to attend (three of which he set up himself): May 4 at Madras High School in Madras, Oregon; May 9 at Marshfield High School in his hometown of Coos Bay, Oregon; May 15 at the British Columbia International Track Meet inside Swangard Stadium, 3883 Imperial Street, Burnaby, British Columbia, Canada; May 24 at the California Relays at Modesto Junior College, 435 College Avenue, Modesto, California; and May 29 at the NCAA Preparation Meet at UO's Hayward Field.

At Madras High School, Prefontaine won the 3,000 meters (8:26.4). After winning the 2,000 meters in an AR 5:01.4 at Coos Bay five days later, he won the 5,000 meters in a MR 13:46.8 at the British Columbia International Track Meet.

On May 24, at the 1975 California Relays, Prefontaine won the two-mile in 8:36.4. He then concluded the Finnish tour with a win on his collegiate home track of Hayward Field, on May 29, in the 5,000 meters (13:23.8) for his twenty-fifth consecutive win in Eugene of races over a mile.

Tragically, about four hours later, he died in a car accident on Skyline Boulevard, just outside UO. He was twenty-four.

The response to the news of his passing was overwhelming and worldwide. It also became apparent that he touched many lives in his short life, and his impact is felt all over Oregon, the United States, and the globe.

Along with the many memorials and monuments that appeared locally in the days, months, and years afterward, about seven years after Prefontaine's passing a relationship developed between Coos Bay and the Chiba Prefecture city of Choshi in Japan.

It all started, inadvertently, in October 1982.

Explained Sasaki Yuko of Choshi City Hall Planning and Finance Department and the Choshi International and Multicultural Association, "The mayor of Choshi city visited Coos Bay city when he went to the U.S. to inspect port facilities, which led to a letter from the mayor of Coos Bay city in December 1982, stating that the Coos Bay City Council had decided to conclude a sister-city agreement. Since Coos Bay city's core industries are agriculture and fisheries, and it has a fishing port and harbor, it has many similarities with Choshi city. Therefore, we responded that we would like to conclude a sister-city agreement with Coos Bay city and proposed to conclude a sister-city agreement at the extraordinary assembly of the city council in January 1983, which was unanimously approved."

In Japan on February 10, 1983, to mark the fiftieth anniversary of when Choshi in 1933 became a city—forty-four years after Choshi was established as a town in 1889—a sister-city-agreement signing ceremony was held and attended by representatives from both cities.

"With Coos Bay city, we have been sending and receiving goodwill delegations; sister-school agreements for elementary school, junior high school, and city high school; a yearlong study-abroad program at a community college; and sending delegations to visit with junior high school and high school students in the city on an irregular basis," Yuko noted.

Representing Coos Bay, former South Coast Development Council executive director Connie Stopher often visited Japan while she was in office.

"Coos Bay has long had a Japanese population and is home to some Japanese businesses," observed Stopher. "That may have been why a relationship was started. Choshi was a good fit because it's also a coastal town with a long history of fishing. In terms of what each does, it's mostly about friendship. In addition to my two trips, Choshi has sent a delegation to visit Coos Bay."

Despite an interruption between the cities, the relationship continues.

"The exchange program was suspended after the September 11 attacks in the U.S. in 2001, and this situation is still continuing today," Yuko said. "Since then, there have been no specific visits or other mutual exchanges, but Coos Bay city extended its sympathy to us after the [2011] Great East Japan Earthquake, and Connie Stopher visited Choshi each time she came to Japan in 2015 and 2016, where we had dinner with the mayor of Choshi and exchanged letters."

Prefontaine Memorial monument in Japan. *Courtesy Choshi International and Multicultural Association/Choshi City Hall.*

In each city, there is also a public park and garden that reflects traditional Japanese horticulture and design.

"Coos Bay has a park called Mingus Park, and within it is the Choshi Gardens," Stopher noted. "It's a beautiful Japanese garden dedicated to Choshi and the sister-city relationship."

In the center of Choshi is Central Green Park, also the site of the Pre Memorial monument, a similar replication of the one situated in Coos Bay.

"The monument, donated by the City of Coos Bay to commemorate the opening of the Central Green Park, was unveiled and opened to the public on April 17, 1986," recalled Yuko. "The monument went through the trouble that the [separate granite stone and plaque] which was a part of it was stolen. However, thanks to Coos Bay city and [a] great contribution by Nike Japan, it reconstructed in May 2015."

Stuart Woods, creator of the Pre Memorial monument in Coos Bay, was involved in the Japan model, which differs slightly from his original.

"The mayor of Choshi City, Chiba Prefecture, Japan, visited the area and was inspired by the story of Steve. They were preparing to construct

Prefontaine Memorial monument in Coos Bay, Oregon. *Photo by Paul Clerici.*

a city park in Choshi in honor of the sister-city relationship. He requested permission to construct a replica of the Prefontaine Memorial, and our local Prefontaine Committee not only agreed but offered to send a duplicate bronze plaque," he said. "I was invited to the dedication of the park and unveiling of their version of the monument [in Japan]. Imagine my surprise when they undraped the Prefontaine Memorial Monument and it was carved out of stone—granite, if I recall. It was a scaled-down version [75 percent] with the plaque mounted on a matching stone base alongside the monument."

# BIBLIOGRAPHY

Bence, Steve. "Random Thoughts and Postings." stevebence.blogspot.com.

Steve Prefontaine Foundation/Prefontaine Memorial Run. www. prefontainerun.com.

U.S. Government Publishing Office. *U.S. Congressional Record—House*. June 10, 1970; July 17, 1975. www.govinfo.gov.

———. *U.S. Congressional Record—Senate*. June 25, 1970; March 13, August 3, 1973; June 10, July 14, 1975. www.govinfo.gov.

———. *U.S. Congress Public Law Statutes 95-606*. 1978. www.govinfo.gov.

———. *U.S. Congress Public Law 36 U.S. Code Chapter 2205*. 1998. www. govinfo.gov.

U.S. Senate. *U.S. Senate Chronological List of Senators*. 2021. www.senate.gov.

Zemper, Eric D., PhD. *The Evolution of Track and Field Rules During the Last Century*. 2008. www.usatfne.org.

# ABOUT THE AUTHOR

**P**aul C. Clerici is the bestselling author of *Born to Coach: The Story of Bill Squires, the Legendary Coach of the Greatest Generation of American Distance Runners* (Meyer + Meyer Sport Publishers) and The History Press books *Images of Modern America: The Boston Marathon*; *A History of the Falmouth Road Race: Running Cape Cod*; *Boston Marathon History by the Mile*; and *History of the Greater Boston Track Club*. He is a journalist, lecturer, media guest, documentary film contributor, writer, photographer, and former newspaper editor and sports editor who has been recognized in the *Marquis Who's Who in the East* publications and received its Albert Nelson Marquis Lifetime Achievement Award. He has written for many newspapers and magazines, including *The Walpole Times*, *Marathon & Beyond*, *Meter*, *New England Patriots Weekly*, *New England Runner*, *Orlando Attractions Magazine*, and *Running Times* among them; and has produced shows at Walpole Community Television. A New England Press Association and Massachusetts Press Association award winner, he was also written for *Running Times/Runner's World*, Strava, and Tracksmith Journal websites/blogs. Race director of the Camy 5K Run & David 5K Walk, he has competed in nearly every distance from the mile to the marathon—including two triathlons and forty-three marathons (the Boston Marathon twenty-three years in a row)—and has won several age-group and Clydesdale awards. A graduate of Curry College in Milton, Massachusetts, the Walpole High School Hall of Fame member resides in his Massachusetts hometown.